SOULMATES ON ICE:
From Hometown Glory to the Top of the Podium

The production of this book was made possible through the generous assistance of the Canada Council of the Arts and the Ontario Arts Council.

Canada Council   Conseil des arts
for the Arts   du Canada

ONTARIO ARTS COUNCIL
CONSEIL DES ARTS DE L'ONTARIO
an Ontario government agency
un organisme du gouvernement de l'Ontario

Library and Archives Canada Cataloguing in Publication

Duhamel, Meagan, 1985-, author
Soulmates on ice : from hometown glory to the top of the podium / by Meagan Duhamel and Eric Radford with Laura E. Young.

Issued in print and electronic formats.
ISBN 978-1-988989-01-3 (softcover).--ISBN 978-1-988989-04-4 (PDF)

1. Duhamel, Meagan, 1985-. 2. Radford, Eric, 1985-. 3. Figure skaters--Ontario--Biography. 4. Autobiographies. I. Young, Laura E., 1963-, author II. Radford, Eric, 1985-, author III. Title.

GV850.A2D84 2018   796.91'20922   C2018-905381-X
                                             C2018-905382-8

Printed and bound in Canada.

Book and Cover design: Heather Campbell and Maurissa Grano
Front cover photo: Danielle Earl/Golden Skate
Meagan Duhamel and Eric Radford back cover photo: Richard Radford

Published by:
Latitude 46 Publishing
info@latitude46publishing.com
Latitude46publishing.com

SOULMATES ON ICE:

From Hometown Glory to the Top of the Podium

By Meagan Duhamel and Eric Radford
with Laura E. Young

LATITUDE 46
PUBLISHING

I had to fall down over one thousand times for this one success.

– Meagan Duhamel, 2018 Olympics

The one who falls and gets up is stronger than the one who never tried.
Do not fear failure but rather fear not trying.

– Roy T. Bennett

They tried to bury us, but they didn't know we are seeds.

– Mexican Proverb

CONTENTS

Introduction

I am trying to avoid Meagan Duhamel's legs as we talk. For someone who is nearly twelve inches shorter than me, she seems to have long legs and they're moving fast and too close to my head for comfort.

We are standing in the warm lobby of Cambrian Arena, buried in central Sudbury on a typical winter night. My sons are practising hockey and after their team leaves, Meagan will skate with the local club. She may be home on vacation from Barrie but she needs to fit in her ice time. The leg swings are part of her warm-up.

By this point in her career, I'd interviewed her several times for *The Sudbury Star*. Now we are just chatting and catching up. It is great to see her and absorb her vibrant energy. But as much as she loves to talk about sport in general, and specifically where her skating is going, she has ice time and there's no lingering. After she heads off, and while my sons are changing, I take a long moment to watch, to see her fly. There she goes.

As a journalist writing in a small city, inevitably one writes about local athletes' early careers: the top results, the singular drive, the moving away, the regional, provincial, Canadian and Olympic teams! You see them off, happy and hopeful for them.

Over time, and along with my colleagues, I have told the story of an incredible legacy of athletes in Sudbury: Alex Baumann, Eric Wohlberg, David Spears, Gary Trevisiol, Devon Kershaw, Rebecca Johnston, Tessa Bonhomme, Eli Pasquale, Robert Esmie, and Denis Vachon and coaches like Gord Apolloni and the late Peter Ennis and Jeno Tihanyi. All Olympians or world champions. Then there is that base row of the athletic pyramid where we find the majority of athletes who do not achieve those lofty Olympic levels, who toil in relative anonymity for the love of sport, but athletes nonetheless.

By 2017 a fading, flecking mural of Alex Baumann, 1984 double Olympic swimming champion, and CEO of Own the Podium through the 2010 Vancouver Olympics, was covered up as part of Laurentian University renovations. It was the second dedication, both on Ramsey Lake Road, that was covered over. Acknowledgement of what he has done in Canadian sport has faded from public view. Now there is only a small display case of photos at the pool where he used to train, sometimes three times a day. Along that same corridor leading to the Jeno Tihanyi Olympic Gold Pool in Sudbury, all that remains of a swimming legend is a shimmering black granite plaque dedicated to honouring all that he and Tihanyi achieved together. In fact there is minimal recognition in the hometown of all these fine Sudbury athletes, part of an unfortunate, collective amnesia when it comes to our appreciation of our athletes.

In January of 2017, Meagan Duhamel's mother Heidi joined aquacise classes at the city pool where I lifeguard part-time. I had to get confirmation of the local legend: did you and your husband work three jobs each to keep things going? It was two. Then we got talking.

When I later learned that Meagan was retiring after the 2018 Olympics I wanted to somehow respect and acknowledge what she had done for sport, at the very least locally. Until 2018 there was really nothing around town that displayed her legacy.

And while we're at it, I thought, let's add to the fine tradition of skating books that exists. Meagan always has a story to tell and she's one of the best athletes to interview, always so available and candid. Yet, there were still questions to explore.

When she hopped onboard the project, naturally we were going to include Eric, as well, which turned out to be a real bonus for this entire book as he also has a story to tell—though it is different, and that has been part of the appeal of writing their story. They are unique people, and unique skaters, yet they are so similar, especially where it matters. In fact their similarities emerge more so than their differences in what is now a Northern Ontario proud project and a story that reflects so much of what it takes to pursue sport in Canada.

My personal appreciation of figure skating lies at the training level where the sport is stripped down to athletes working hard, not so much the dressed-up side and the judging issues. As one skating parent explained, skaters are like swimmers. The amount of time they spend training in their sport is inversely proportional to the amount of time of the performance.

What was it then about skating that appealed to Meagan and Eric? How did they prove themselves so worthy of the sport, when their road to success was riddled with bumps and potholes? As is so often the case with stories of great achievement, those obstacles along their way are what made their story so compelling.

And so, a few years after that leg-side encounter with Meagan, she didn't make the 2006 or 2010 Olympic teams. After each time, she was finding a way with a new partner, a new training site. Really? You're not retired? Haven't you had enough already?

In 2012 I met Meagan with Eric Radford for the first time. They were backstage for a skating show tour early in their partnership. Off-ice they looked tight, solid—a real friendship back then, even though they did lack some energy on the ice.

Then they were off to the Olympics in 2014 where they won a silver in the team event. They were twice world champions. Then they finished seventh in the world and endured a rocky 2016–2017 season. When we began working on their story, we didn't know how the Olympic season would unfold and that lent a sense of mystery to a sports story.

They retired from skating having completed the dream of four near perfect performances on the world's biggest stage. The conclusion of their competitive careers reminded me of the ending of a long summer day when daylight holds on, seemingly forever. Then, just as the sun sets over the blue lake, with its rocky Northern shore, gold light bursts across the horizon, capping the wonderful, long day. For Eric and Meagan, that light shimmered gold

Meagan Duhamel and Eric Radford with Laura E. Young

and bronze at the 2018 Winter Olympics. As they did their job, could they have written a better ending to their story?

With a complete set of Olympic medals, Meagan and Eric are the two most successful, enduring skaters to emerge from Northern Ontario. For the North, who knows when it will be our turn again?

On a larger scale, they are part of a generation of skaters that emerged after the 90s–00s wave of skaters, the après Kurt Browning: Elvis Stojko, Isabelle Brasseur and Lloyd Eisler, Jamie Salé and David Pelletier, Joannie Rochette, even Skate Canada Team Manager Michael Slipchuk.

Meagan and Eric, Patrick Chan in men's singles, and likely ice dancers Tessa Virtue and Scott Moir are all retiring to trace new paths in skating, but if history is anything in Canadian skating, the sport should be fine.

No one would have placed Meagan and Eric even in this conversation when they were first paired in what were possibly the dying days of their skating careers in 2010.

They both left Northern Ontario reluctantly to pursue their passion for skating, finally settling in Montreal. When they were twenty-five and twenty-six years old, the opportunity came to retire. Instead, their skating careers were revived when they were paired early in 2010. What did it take to stay in a sport for so long, and then to make it late in a long skating career? Why indeed was it worth it when, in a judged sport on thin blades, victory is never a guarantee?

Although this is Meagan and Eric's story we also hear from others closest to them, their families and coaches. At times, they speak as one team, one solid unit; other times, their voices separate, sometimes because pairs do skate apart in their routines, others because there was a disconnect during their lowest point after the 2016–2017 season. How did they get from that rock bottom to the top of the Olympic podium and a storybook ending less than a year later in February 2018?

In order to tell the story, we interviewed in person and over Skype. Their final competitive season was intensely busy, but, like everything else in their skating careers, somehow even this book project was made to work. Most interviews occurred in the same time zone.

In September 2017 I watched them train in Sainte-Julie, when they were trying to iron out the bugs in the underwhelming long program to an otherwise uplifting medley of songs by British rock band Muse. They would, unsurprisingly, jettison this Muse long program in December.

As I watched from rinkside, trying to overhear the comments from choreographer Julie Marcotte, it was hard to believe that anyone ever thought Meagan and Eric didn't look right skating together. That's how it seems to be in Canadian pairs skating: odd matches often work out for the best and most were singles skaters before transferring over to pairs. When Meagan and Eric came to pairs skating by 2006, with different partners and after moderately successful singles careers, they were joining the strong tradition of unusual and ultimately successful Canadian pairs.

Even though she was about to set a record, winning her seventh Canadian pairs title in 2018, Meagan would say that all the pairs who came before had done great work in their careers. It wasn't so much that she and Eric had made it "better," Meagan reflected. Instead, they followed that legacy and pushed the envelope of technical expertise to shake up their sport, in a proud Canadian tradition.

Pairs skating is perhaps the ultimate merging of athletic talent. Pairs skating debuted in the Olympics in 1952, but unlike Russia, Canada has not produced perennial gold medallists. Sometimes Canadian pairs have suffered at the Olympics, only to return and win the World Figure Skating Championships (Worlds) one month later, as Barbara Underhill and Paul Martini did so famously after the 1984 Olympics.

The 2002 Olympic champions Jamie Salé and David Pelletier skated together for four years and won twelve of thirteen competitions, as well as the Olympics. It was the last time a Canadian pair would win a gold medal at the Olympics. Their Olympic experience also fast-tracked the massive overhaul of the scoring and judging system from the infamous 6.0 to the graded, computerized system that is now shown in real time, at least for the technical elements, as the skaters' programs are performed.

On the night of the actual event in 2002 in Salt Lake City, Salé and Pelletier won silver but their performance was felt to be the best of the night. In the ensuing uproar over the tight defeat to Elena Bereznaya and Anton Sikharulidze, their talented Russian rivals, a judging scandal and collusion were laid bare. Scores were thrown out, and since Salé and Pelletier were now tied with Bereznaya and Sikharulidze, the two pairs teams were re-awarded a shared gold medal in one of the most awkward, unsatisfying medal ceremonies the Olympics has seen. The two teams rapidly turned pro, and Salé and Pelletier flew to vacation in Hawaii a few weeks later.

The days of the 6.0 were numbered, anyway. The new system, the International Judging System, was adopted in 2004 and fully implemented internationally by the next Olympic season, 2005–2006 and the 2006 Winter Olympics in Torino. Now a panel of nine judges scores skaters on technical merit and presentation, for a combined final score breakdown from each judge. At the end, skaters receive a score sheet so they can review their details. The scores are available online now after every event. It's a system that Meagan and Eric employed to their advantage to help push the technical envelope.

Supreme technical skill seems to be part of the Canadian skating gift to the world.

In the 1950s, Frances Dafoe and Norris Bowden landed the first throw jump, catch lift, twist lift, and overhead lasso lift in the world, now considered the "staples" of pairs. They would win three world titles, and Olympic pairs silver in 1956. Barbara Wagner and Robert Paul won four consecutive world titles and became the first non-Europeans to win pairs skating when they claimed gold at the 1960 Olympics. En route to winning the 1962 Worlds, Maria and Otto Jelinek became the first pairs team in the world to complete lifts with several rotations, now staples of pairs skating. In 1964, Debbi Wilkes and Guy Revell were second at the Olympics.

By the 1980s, Underhill and Martini went into the Sarajevo Olympics in 1984 as favourites. They had a noticeable size difference but appealed anyway and won five Canadian championships. After finishing seventh, they almost retired. Legend has it that 1984 Olympic silver medallist and two-time world champion and Underhill's dear friend, Brian Orser, suggested she return to an old pair of skates.

The old skates worked: Underhill and Martini finished their careers by winning the world championship on Canadian ice in Ottawa. They retired to enjoy a long career as professionals, winning seven world titles, and skating with Ice Capades and Stars on Ice. They were inducted into the World Figure Skating Hall of Fame in 2009.

Watching that inspiring skate in 1984 was a twelve-year-old Isabelle Brasseur, a promising pairs skater from Quebec. Eventually partnered with the taller Lloyd Eisler, she became a three-time Olympian, won two bronze medals in the 1992 and 1994 Olympics, the world title in 1993, and three world medals.

The skating community is a small one. Isabelle is now a pairs skating coach in New Jersey with her husband, Rocky Marval, who also skated pairs. Isabelle coaches their daughter, Gabriella, and makes the occasional trip north to Montreal to visit Bruno Marcotte, who also coached Meagan and Eric.

For Isabelle, pairs partnerships hold a hint of mystery, much in the way a marriage's inner workings may not be obvious to the outside world. The pairs bond is tinged with intrigue: do they like each other? Respect each other? Are they friends? Could they be lovers? If not, what is their connection?

Isabelle, who is also close friends with Julie Marcotte, Eric and Meagan's choreographer, says she and Lloyd also weren't a match made in skating heaven. She was small and bright, he was tall and dark. On the ice, they were technically oriented, unlike Underhill and Martini who were so smooth that their edges melted, and Salé and Pelletier, who were a mix of the two, she says.

"What matters are respect, communication and having the same goals. Those things make you a strong unit, so that no matter what life throws your way, you'll get through it. You'll adjust to anything.

"No pair is perfect: they all have different life and skating struggles that up-and-coming athletes can relate to if they take the time to read the story. They would realize, 'Hey, I'm not perfect either, but they survived it, they pushed through it and they managed to get on top. So could I.' "

It wasn't Underhill and Martini's win in Ottawa that night that was so amazing, Isabelle says. "They overcame a major obstacle in their career and they managed to handle everything around them to come back and win and be the best they can be."

Throughout her career, despite often not succeeding at her goals, Isabelle would tell herself she should keep going until she knew she had done her best. That was the example she took from Underhill and Martini.

"Maybe all the young teams are seeing Meagan and Eric, and hopefully every so often, there's a Canadian team that stays on top and shows that example to kids. That if you keep fighting, you'll make it, too."

Meagan and Eric restored the technical side of pairs skating in their own way that had to do with their personal dynamic, Isabelle says. Eric is smooth with long, classical lines and edges, while Meagan packs the technical punch and is more muscular, she says.

"Their coaches took that blend, the two skaters with different styles, and created something amazing in meshing their qualities together."

Meagan and Eric pushed the technical equation to a whole new level, "probably more than what anyone could have dreamed in the pairs world," says Isabelle.

Their legacy is found in the way they analyzed and planned their programs, upping the technical game for all pairs skaters. Now juniors have to compete with triple Salchows and triple toe loop jumps, the relatively "easier" jumps, while at the senior level, the triple Lutz and flip now appear. Not to mention the throw quadruple Salchow. "It's crazy the quads she does," Isabelle adds of Meagan.

In the beginning the difference in style between the two was a hard sell for some, but Meagan and Eric knew it would work, Isabelle says. "They put their hearts and souls into what they do. Obviously when they stepped on the ice together the first few times, they felt that light inside that their match would work."

Isabelle hopes that the special pairs elements, the death spirals, the spins and lifts will remain as important as the side-by-side jumps. "In the end, if you want to be top in the world, you have to be able to do a little bit of everything, not just one or the other."

Most of all, the female partner must love to fly, and she must do so by blending her power with that of her partner. The woman takes flight in pairs thanks to the power of someone often twice her size. "And if you don't love that, you won't love pairs," she adds, laughing.

✦

On a winter's night long ago, I was interviewing Heather Duhamel, Meagan's sister, about her skating at an upcoming event. We were rinkside, and other Walden Figure Skating Club athletes were still milling around in their outfits, skating their elements effortlessly. Sometimes sport is at its best at this community level and its simplest, like a basic cartwheel, or a single Lutz jump.

As I talked to Heather, this one skater kept spinning and jumping. She wasn't rude about it, nor was she pushy. But she knew exactly where to skate so that she was lodged in my peripheral vision and gaining my attention.

Instead of ignoring her or being frustrated (You're interrupting the interview!), I watched, intrigued, for a few minutes. Eventually, I asked, "Who's that?"

Oh, that's Heather's little sister, I was told by another skater. I thought, "Well, that's impressive. She has a lot of energy."

I recalled that moment the next time I heard about Meagan and skating. And the next ...

THE FIRST PERFECT SKATE

And so for about five minutes I go all fan-girl and enjoy the fact that I'm watching Meagan and Eric train at their new home base in Sainte-Julie, on Montreal's south shore, just after Labour Day 2017. They both appear separately to greet me this September morning and manage to get the interview done wedged in between the focused routine and lifestyle of the elite athlete.

In this case there are added features specific to Meagan and Eric: one of Meagan's puppies was sick overnight and now has to go to the vet; Eric has his osteopath appointment as part of the vital maintenance required to keep his back healthy for the Olympic season.

Arena Ste-Julie is nondescript, with nothing fancy to indicate that it's home to an elite skating school. It's just the basics: ice, boards, stands. There is a pile of crash pads in the corner; one assumes for the short track speed skaters who train here.

You're quickly reminded about one truth of figure skating: that there is nothing between the ice and the skater falling on it. After watching one fifty-minute training session I'm close to tossing a couple of crash pads over the glass to where one skater keeps falling. Over and over she jumps; over and over she falls.

Falls are rare even in practice for Meagan and Eric. It's an interesting time, perhaps a crossroads for them. Their 2016–2017 season just ended in injuries, frustrations, falling from first in the world to seventh. They've left Richard Gauthier, one of their main coaches, who was also instrumental in their careers, their pairing, and their two world titles. There is a sense of anticipation in the air—over the Olympics, over the unknown path their season will follow. Professionally, I am secretly planning for two writing scenarios: off the podium in the Olympics or complete satisfaction with four ideal performances and on the podium.

And so, the 2016 World Championships in Boston seems like a logical place to begin—a happier time, when they won with that elusive perfect skate.

They settle in, on break between their morning and afternoon sessions. They quickly check omnipresent phones and then write cheques to pay for club membership. They sit with Meagan slightly in the foreground, Eric behind in the practised order of skating pairs.

"When I think about the perfect skate we had in Boston—I didn't try to have a perfect skate or make any emotion happen," Meagan recalls. "It was completely organic, natural. That's when the emotion is real and that's usually when the magic can happen. When you try to force it to happen, it never works."

Leading up to a skate it's all about dealing with waves of nerves, anxiety and expectations, Eric reflects.

"I feel ready, I know that we can do this, I'm just going to enjoy the moment. Then there are moments where it feels like the world is ending and I can't. This is way too difficult for me to do right now."

That 2015–2016 season had been tricky. For the first time in their careers they were the team to chase, whereas most of their skating lives they had thrived on striving and flying in the face of anyone who ever thought they shouldn't be skating together.

In Boston they are sitting second, behind Sui Wenjing and Han Cong of China.

Meagan and Eric practised that morning in Boston, then waited over eight hours for the actual competition. It was a long time, between practice and competition as they tried to rest back at the hotel.

Meagan found meditation helpful for keeping her mind in the moment where she needed to be. She can visualize pretty much everything and anything but sometimes what she sees is a skater's worst nightmare: falling on choreography, missing spins.

"There's so much that can happen in your mind and it didn't matter if we were skating at a big or small competition. We always want to have our best skate. We have high expectations of ourselves," she says.

They can have the big moment, the perfect skate on the dimly lit ice with its grey corners in Sainte-Julie. But the real challenge is doing it in the moment on the world's biggest stage.

"That's what creates the most anxiety or nervousness, knowing that the moment we want to have is possible," Eric says. "It's up to us, to each of us individually and as partners in a split second to make sure it happens the way we've been imagining, dreaming and hoping. That happens everywhere in life, not just in skating."

Eric recalls how a sense of detachment can sometimes help. At the 2012 Worlds in Nice, France, they had finished warming up and were walking backstage when Eric happened to look out a window and see someone walking their dog. "They were so far removed and unaware of what I'm going through in my life right now. I'm about to go on the ice at the World Championships and do this incredibly difficult routine."

Then he imagined what would happen if he just up and walked away, disappearing. "Sometimes just having a random thought like that can remove me from the big, intense pressure that I'm under."

Knowing what they are capable of creates the most apprehension before skating. But after the waves of emotion settle, they feel a calm sea of readiness where they will enjoy the moment and the view.

Usually the World Championships are the pinnacle of the long skating season. By this point, the skaters know each other's order of elements, their music, the energy of the audience. The audience is not to be ignored. On a perfect night, the skaters are both part of that energy, and yet so far out of it.

Backstage Meagan ties and reties her skates, too loose, too tight. Eric sips from a cup of coffee, eats a banana and a protein bar. Meagan eats a banana. They might, of course, check their phones. Just prior to the six-minute warm-up for the final flight of skaters, Eric sprays grip on his hands.

Sui and Han skated before the Canadians. They skated well, but it felt like the crowd still had the capacity to really be wowed. And so in Boston, the Canadians set out with the usual stress, pressure and nerves, but coated with confidence, Meagan recalls. "That covering of confidence allows you to settle. It's a perfect combination."

"When we've had really good skates I always describe having a little ball of yes in my stomach," Eric adds. "The nervous energy is going all over the place, up my shoulders, up my chest and heart but below all that in the pit of my stomach is this little ball: you're going to do it."

Then Meagan and Eric step out, their performance flowing. They begin their mental checklist: okay, we're just stepping on the ice now. Okay we're putting one foot in front of the other. Okay our music is going to play. Okay we're going to do our choreography. Okay, we're going to do a triple twist. "It's like each moment is so isolated in time," Meagan says.

The lead-off element, the throw triple twist, was wonky but Meagan wasn't rattled as she landed. "It was, 'Okay I'll do the next thing.' When I'm in the zone something can go wrong and I'm okay. It's like an energy."

"You get into this zone. If there are little blips, you return to the wave," Eric adds.

The layout of their program was such that Eric had Meagan high overhead in the final lift. As they rounded the corner, they could see that their coaches Bruno and Richard were celebrating wildly. That got Meagan going, yelling along with them.

"Right when it finished—we're always imagining that moment. Is it real? It almost feels like it could be a dream. It's not just like you feel proud of what you did, you feel relief because you're done. There's so much energy in the room. It's all the best emotions rolled into one," Eric says.

"Usually our families are in the arena. We're sharing the moment with our coaches, everybody who's been on this journey with us. The best feelings are right then and there when you're like, 'Wow, we did it,'" Meagan says.

On paper, Meagan and Eric won their second consecutive world title by seven points, their season's best score by ten points. It was the fourth year in a row they had landed on the world podium.

For Eric and Meagan the ultimate of possibilities had happened. Of all the things that could have gone wrong that day, they had actually made it happen in the best way, in the most difficult moment of all.

"It's the same for every athlete. But when we look back, when we were taking our starting position, everyone had the same opportunity we did but we were the ones who made it happen in that moment and skated the best we could," Eric says.

"We've won all these titles. But the titles are not fun to win unless you have those moments. We've won a lot of competitions where we don't skate as well, and they're not as magical. There's nothing really fulfilling about them. It's really that magic of the perfect skate which is the beauty of being able to win," Meagan says.

The music that year? "Hometown Glory" by Adele.

We wrap up the interview as the ice is resurfaced before the afternoon training session begins. On this humid September day in 2017, the skies were overcast across Montreal. The radio was alive with warnings about looming delays in Montreal traffic, as if that is news.

It seemed weird to be in an ice rink when it was summer outside, and going to the rink should be put off until the last minute. With the notoriously long Canadian winters, everyone is indoors enough as it is.

At the time, this conversation was just a general reflection on a perfect skate for two skaters entering what they had announced would be their final competitive season. It felt like a good place to start.

What none of us realized then was that their last season represented the first brush strokes of the masterpiece that is their career, and that they would ultimately return to "Hometown Glory."

2010: IS MY CAREER OVER?

There was a feeling of fatigue at the end of the 2009–2010 season.

Eric and Rachel Kirkland had ended their partnership of four years after finishing seventh at the 2009 Canadians. They had been training part-time with pairs coach Ingo Steuer, of Germany, who was the 1998 Olympic bronze medallist with Mandy Wötzel, and with Brian Orser, who was primarily a singles coach, though as skating fans know, he is not your average singles coach.

With his parents, Eric had discussed leaving Canada to skate for Germany, which meant he would also become a German citizen. Ingo would find him a partner in Germany. There seemed to be no one to skate with in Canada and Eric didn't know what else to do but up and move to Germany. "That's how much he loved skating. He couldn't find the right partner," Eric's mom Valerie Radford recalls.

At one time it was what they had to do for his skating, and they had let Eric move from Balmertown to Kenora, then Winnipeg, then Montreal, and finally back to Toronto. He and Rachel had been training part-time and had even competed in the 2009 German National Championships in the international entries, finishing second. They were seventh at the 2009 Canadians.

This potential move to Europe was now too much and too far. So Eric's parents laid out some options: call Skate Canada or call Richard Gauthier who was in charge of a renowned pairs skating school in Montreal with Bruno Marcotte and his sister, choreographer Julie Marcotte. Rick and Valerie didn't really know Richard, but Eric knew Bruno.

Rick and Valerie were living in Bermuda and flew to Montreal to talk with Richard Gauthier. Valerie was honest, telling Richard that they were all at the end of their collective rope, emotionally, financially. They were all looking outside the rink to retirement and what lay beyond. But at twenty-six, Eric was looking for the right pairs partner so he moved back to Montreal.

As Eric recalls, he began the 2010 Olympic season glad just to be in Montreal where he was teamed with his third partner, Anne-Marie Giroux, who hailed from Quebec.

"That year I was just so happy to have made the change from my prior situation, happy to have a new partner and be with an actual pairs coach. Up to that point I didn't have a full-time pairs coach.

"It was refreshing to be in Montreal. I had just left a relationship, though, so it was also a difficult time. I had stopped skating with Rachel. It was like a clean slate.

"Heading into the 2010 Olympic trials, of course I had the dream of going to the Vancouver Olympics but I knew it was quite improbable. Anne-Marie and I were a new team. Technically we weren't as strong as we needed to be to compete with the top teams. Beyond the Olympics it would have been nice to aim for a national team which would have meant a top five finish at Canadians [Canadian Figure Skating Championships] that year. We'd have to skate cleanly."

At Canadians, Eric and Anne-Marie skated decently enough and received compliments on their programs. But during their short program, they fell on the double Axel and that was the end of even being able to entertain any hint of the Olympic dream. They were eighth and Canada was only sending two teams to the Vancouver Olympics. They didn't even make the national team. Eric wondered if it was time to face the real world.

"I remember talking to a friend and crying before going to bed. I really didn't know what I was supposed to be doing. I put my parents under so much financial stress. I felt completely lost in my life. It was really horrible.

"When the Olympics opened in Vancouver, I felt so disheartened that I didn't want to be in Canada. I went to Australia to visit my brother Richard who was a chiropractor there. I remember flying through New York City and at the airport watching Yuna Kim skate. I saw the gold medal hockey game. That was great. But it was just nice to get away.

"Ingo had told me once, 'You're going to skate with Tatiana Volosozhar.' Of course, I was super excited because she was the best pairs skater in the world, then. I always felt that I could be one of the best male pairs skaters in the world but I had to find the right partner. Ingo said that really secretively to me. It's so long ago now. But it was something I used to contemplate. Would I want to give up my whole life to go and skate with Tatiana? It was a really big decision. Financing was a factor. It was too big of a decision to make."

Eric felt so hopeful about his own skating. "I thought I had the ability, and with the right partner I could get to where I wanted to go," Eric says. He figures the issue was always a lack of circumstances rather than a lack of ability. But he wondered if he had a future in skating. Maybe it wasn't in the cards. He had seen it happen before; so many talented people come and go in the sport and don't achieve what they want to. He was starting to think that maybe it was time to go to school, study music and composition. He was considering university and thought about returning to Toronto. He was ready to move on.

In 2009, Meagan Duhamel was training with her second partner, Craig Buntin, who was skating to compete at the 2010 Olympics in his hometown of Vancouver before retiring. Meagan assumed she would retire when Craig did. After teaming up in 2007, Meagan and Craig became three-time national medallists, 2010 Four Continents Figure Skating Championships bronze medallists, and finished sixth at the 2008 Worlds.

But it was a painful time: Craig's rotator cuff, labrum and three tendons were a torn, tangled mess. He needed eight months to heal enough to be able to lift Meagan. Then there were Meagan's injuries heading into the critical months prior to the 2010 Olympics. The pain started in her lower back and evolved into two stress fractures and a herniated disc. Meagan says she let the injury be.

"I really didn't have time for something like this. I saw a physio a couple of times. It just slowly got worse. I was getting so stiff. It hurt if I coughed or sneezed. I couldn't find a comfortable position to rest.

"Then I started to get this tingling pain down my right leg and complete weakness in my muscles. I could not activate my muscles. This was all starting to blow up in November 2009. It was like my leg was asleep and tingling. It was like I was walking on a piece of wood. But given the Olympic qualification was coming in January, I didn't have much choice. I had to find a way to push through it.

"Once I finally struggled out of bed in the morning, I lay in the shower and let the hot water pour over me. That would slowly start to loosen all the muscles. Then I'd be able to move a little bit. But sometimes I'd bend over to tie my shoe and I'd be stuck. I couldn't get up. It was like, 'Oh, crap.' Then I'd have to hold a wall and push myself up."

Sometimes when Meagan was skating, she would jump or do a lift and get stuck in that position. She couldn't win. Whatever helped her stress fracture aggravated the herniated disc and made it worse. Arching her back helped one and made the other worse. She was in a constant state of discomfort and taking a lot of medication. Of course she continued training and never stopped jumping.

In between training sessions, during the ten-minute break to resurface the ice, she would sit in the change room, and when she tried to get up again, she couldn't move. Again, she was holding onto the wall to lift herself back up. The constant pain became the new normal for Meagan. She had to take her time getting up. For Meagan this was just another road block to navigate.

"In hindsight, if I'd known what was in store for me in the future with Eric, I would have not skated. I would have taken the time off that I needed in order to be healthy again, and stayed away from the Olympic qualification.

"But I was determined I was going to qualify for the Olympics, I was going to go to the Olympics and then skating would be over. I would have been at Worlds and the Olympics and it would have been amazing. I would have had an amazing career because I had never dreamed of winning medals at these competitions. It was just enough for me to compete at Canadians and Worlds.

"By December doctors were thinking they had to freeze my back. I had no time to take a couple of days off to let the freezing set. And I was so scared of getting the injection. The pain of that procedure seemed about the same as the pain I was living through."

The Olympics were so close, right in front of her, and she was going to do whatever it took to get there. She didn't stop skating, and even managed to skate really well at the Olympic qualification.

The Canadians were held in London in January. Meagan and Craig had finished second in 2009, so they were in the mix to qualify for Vancouver. The Duhamel family drove the five hour trip south to watch.

Just before Meagan and Craig skated, Joannie Rochette's coach, Manon Perron, knew just what to say to inspire Meagan. She looked at Meagan and said, "I'm going to the Olympics so if you want to come with me, get out there and skate well." Energized, Meagan went out to attack the program.

Meagan and Craig opened strongly with a triple jump, hop, triple jump combination and their twist. They fell on the double Axel. They had skated a great short program but still lagged a few points behind second place. When they fell on that Axel in the free skate, in that moment Meagan's heart shattered. They needed to skate cleanly to make it to Vancouver.

"Somehow, despite the fall, we continued the rest of the long program and skated really well. I had hope. I had prepared myself that if we came third, it was okay. I tried to prepare for that blow. I still believed if we skated a great program we could fight for it and get it. The first bit of that program I thought, 'Wow. We are really going to do this.'

"When we went to the double Axel I was so focused on myself, but as soon as I landed and saw Craig beside me it was like, 'Oh, this is over.' I felt it right then and there and it was confirmed when we received our scores. My mom doesn't usually remember statistics and numbers but 109 sticks forever in her mind. That was our score. I ran to find my mother in the concourse. I was sobbing that our score wasn't enough. I had failed to qualify for the Olympics."

A week later Meagan and Craig headed with the rest of the non-Olympic qualifiers to the Four Continents in Jeonju, South Korea. In any other year, it's a great event for skaters. Even for new skaters at the start of their careers. But it's not great if you haven't made the Olympic team, Meagan says.

"I didn't want to go to that Four Continents, but there was prize money we could win and one more chance to compete well. We won the bronze. After that, I went home to Sudbury and Lively to begin the healing process for my back injuries."

"I don't blame not qualifying for the 2010 Olympics on my injury. But I learned a lot about my body. I'd been a vegan since 2008, but this time I explored the wellness world even deeper. I actually never broke my diet when I was injured. I started studying holistic nutrition. I took vitamins to help my nervous system. I tried acupuncture, Pilates and yoga." She went to see Shawn Charron for athletic therapy.

"I resolved that I would never let my body shut me down the way that it had for Vancouver. I was going to do everything I could so that my body could handle whatever was coming my way."

Once Meagan's back started to feel better she started running. Otherwise she didn't skate. She watched the Vancouver Olympics that February on TV from her couch. At the end of March she watched the Worlds, and felt like she should have been there representing Canada in Italy. A feeling was brewing—one that she didn't want to live with for the rest of her life. She imagined telling people, 'Yeah, I was the alternate twice for the Olympics. And I almost qualified but I didn't. I just stopped.' She didn't want to have any regrets.

"During that time, I just didn't want to be in pain anymore. But as my injuries started to heal, something odd happened. Every time I came up with a reason why I didn't want to skate, or think, 'Oh, I never have to do a long program again,' something would tell me, 'Oh, but you like doing a long program. It gives you a sense of pride after a great long program.' I could always find a reason against quitting skating. The pros for skating cancelled the cons on so many occasions.

"I was exhausted, mentally, physically, emotionally. As soon as the emotional and mental exhaustion faded, everything seemed more seamless in my recovery.

"I have never felt like I missed anything in my life. I loved the path I had chosen to take. The beginning of my partnership with Craig was so amazing. We started skating together and all of a sudden I was achieving all these things I'd only dreamt of doing. I was winning medals at Canadians. I had a Team Canada jacket and I was at Worlds and I was having all these great skates. It was exciting.

"Then it stopped being exciting. We raised our expectations, then we couldn't get along. He was injured. I was injured. It was fun for the first year and it quickly died. I wondered whether I would put myself through all that again. Why would I do that at twenty-five years old? What's the point? Going to the Olympics is not worth it if that's what it takes.

"Looking back at it now, if Craig and I had qualified for the 2010 Olympics, we would have probably finished between tenth and fifteenth. That would have been amazing—I would have gone to the Olympics and I would have retired. I would have not experienced what I am now. It really puts it into perspective. I really believe everything happens for a reason. I really believe that more now than ever because I've experienced so many great things through skating. I definitely would have felt so fulfilled. I'm glad this happened to me in 2010 because it changed my life. You don't realize at it the time."

Meagan Duhamel and Eric Radford with Laura E. Young

OUR FAMILIES SPEAK ABOUT SKATING

Eric is seven years old and figure skating is on TV in his living room. As he jumps and twirls, he tells his parents that so-and-so from Russia has just completed a triple Lutz triple toe jump in combination.

"Rick and I would look at each other and say, 'What's a triple Lutz triple toe?' At a young age he really knew his jumps, knew these peoples' names," Valerie Radford recalls.

And Eric knew he wanted to add skating to his already packed athletics schedule.

Lakes, rocks, and trees rule the vast geography that is Northern Ontario. The scattered small towns seem to be carved out in some pre-determined way, with just enough space parcelled out before their borders blur with the wilderness. Even to this day, Northern Ontario still feels wild, deeply green, and ever-expanding.

It was here, in the freedom of all that space, that Eric began his skating career.

When he wasn't jumping and imitating the skaters he watched on TV, Eric would chase his brother Richard around the open-area that comprised the living room and the kitchen. "They would drive me crazy!" Valerie remembers.

Growing up in the Balmertown-Red Lake area—about eleven kilometres separate the two towns—Eric was a gangly child, who could ski, play baseball, swim, and tumble across the floor in gymnastics. He skated three times a week but ice time was limited and, especially in the 1990s, was mostly reserved for hockey practice.

Besides, there were so many other sports to try. "The thing is it's a very small area. As a parent it's easy to put your kid in all these sports," Valerie says. "It was busy."

There was a swing set in the garden and in the winter, snowmobiles to ride when the boys were older. At the time, Balmertown really was a small town of about a thousand people, Valerie remembers. The boys had absolute freedom to roam. It was so very safe.

In 1990 when Eric was five, the family moved to Australia for a year. They swam with Imbil Swim Club north of Brisbane. "Eric really came along as a swimmer that year. Then when we went back to Canada, he didn't swim as competitively as Richard. But Eric didn't have time."

Once they were back in Balmertown, Eric was finding his passion for skating above all else. "One day he said, 'Mom. I'm not learning what I want to learn. I want to do jumps.'"

With her husband Rick chuckling in the background, Valerie readily admits she didn't know much about figure skating, especially in the beginning. Red Lake only offered CanSkate lessons. But in a small town, connections were fast and easy. The woman who ran the cafeteria at the high school had a daughter who skated. They talked and were told that Eric would need to take private lessons. She hadn't known there was such a thing.

She asked around at the rink and enrolled Eric in private lessons, joining the Balmertown Figure Skating Club. He eventually became a student of Debra Geary, who was his coach for the first four years of his skating career. By the time he was twelve, Eric could land his double jumps.

At that time Eric asked about where the Canadian Figure Skating Championships were and his mother didn't know. She asked around again and was told Eric wasn't eligible to compete in Canadians because he wasn't even skating in the competitive stream; he was in recreational—not for much longer, however.

Eric began competing in the interclub stream, but in Grade 7 he was already looking further afield. He mentioned a move to Barrie, and the Mariposa Skating School—at that time it was the preeminent skating school in Ontario, and arguably in Canada. "I said, 'You're crazy. You're not going to Barrie,'" Valerie recalls.

But the inevitable was approaching rapidly and so were the even longer trips away to follow Eric's skating. In 1997 they were all at a skating competition in Dryden, when they met up with Rosie Robertson, who was from Kenora and had billeted Richard for swimming. Rosie told the Radfords that Eric could come live with her family if he wanted to skate in Kenora. She had a daughter who skated and Eric knew her.

So in Grade 9, in 1998, thirteen-year-old Eric moved southwest to Kenora, a three-hour drive away. Barrie was too far but now Kenora, at only 260-plus kilometres away, that was reasonable. His parents let him go.

"He seemed to know what he wanted. I've always listened to him when it comes to skating because I didn't know anything about it," Valerie says. "When he said this is what he wanted to do, we've always tried to support him."

In Kenora, Eric lucked out, finding a good home with good people. Rosie Robertson's daughter was the same age as Eric. The two school boards had amalgamated into a bigger unit which may have meant nothing to a teenager, but it meant that Eric could come home every weekend. Two women worked in Kenora and drove home to Balmertown every weekend, bringing Eric with them. They returned him to Kenora on Sundays.

"It's hard to let your kid go, but, I don't know, you get used to travelling these distances in the North," Valerie says, matter-of-factly. She has long known that separation comes with the territory, especially in Northwestern Ontario where the distances seem beyond the comprehension of even those in the Northeast.

They found other ways to see Eric and participate in his life in person. "For parents' night in the school, we would hop in the car right after school was over, drive down to Kenora, and see the teachers." Rick and Valerie would drive back to Red Lake and be at work in the morning.

Richard swam competitively until he was fifteen but beyond that, there was no more competitive swimming for him in Balmertown and Red Lake. There was an opportunity to move to Winnipeg to swim where a club and a billet were waiting. He declined in order to stay home with his friends and play high school sports. "I was kind of surprised because I thought if anybody would have moved away, it would have been Richard and not Eric," Valerie reflects.

After a year in Kenora, Eric moved west to Winnipeg, Manitoba in 1999. Later that year, they followed Eric west to Kelowna, B.C., four provinces away, for Canadians. The drive home was thirty-one hours, with minimal stops. The trip started in pouring rain, which turned into snow as they crossed the Rocky Mountains. The highway closed behind them due to weather, just as they entered Alberta. Then, miraculously, the weather held clear from Calgary home to Red Lake. They returned Eric and his coach Terri Studholme to Winnipeg and continued on another five and half hours or so back to Red Lake. "Life in the North," Valerie says.

Not that any of this was easy. In 2000, the Northern Ontario Sectionals were held in Sault Ste. Marie, a mere 1,250 kilometres southeast of Red Lake. The highway winds along the shores of Lake Superior.

"There was a snowstorm of snowstorms. We got home at 6 o'clock in the morning. We thought we'd be back by midnight." They showered and went to work. "We've had some stories about driving. When we retired we said, 'we're never driving at night.' And we're never driving again in the snow."

As Eric's skating career blossomed, so did the distances between home and his home ice. In 2000, he moved to Montreal to train with Paul Wirtz, who had coached his brother Kris Wirtz and sister-in-law Kristy Sargeant to a Canadian title, and the world stage.

By 2001 Eric was at least back in Ontario, having followed his coach to the Cricket Club in Toronto. Richard was just further south studying kinesiology at the University of Windsor. In September 2002 he began studying at the Canadian Memorial Chiropractic College in Toronto. That same month, Valerie began working in Toronto. After four years of parenting Eric over the phone, and with Richard now in Toronto, Valerie and Rick enjoyed a few years where they would live as a family. They all moved onto the main floor of a rented house in Toronto together.

"We used to call Eric's room the Harry Potter room, that's how small it was," Valerie says.

"I don't care," Eric would say. "I'm with you guys."

Rick was unemployed for a year. "It was a very, very difficult situation. Skating is expensive. I didn't have a job. I was wearing down my RRSPs. I had no pension."

In 2006 Rick, a mining inspector, found work in Bermuda. Eric was twenty-one and able to be on his own. Richard graduated from chiropractic college in June 2006 and moved to Australia to work. In 2012 he would return to Red Lake and open Sunrise Chiropractic.

Valerie retired from teaching in Canada in 2006, a year past her retirement date. She continued to work for five years, while they were in Bermuda. "I thought I was going to have to work until I was one hundred to pay off our figure skating debt," she laughs.

They had viewed great swaths of Canada on their journeys but owned none of it. They had been told that one parent usually moves with the skater to live, but the Radfords wondered how the family could afford the skater's training that way. "We were not wealthy. When we were in this, a lot of our friends would not have done what we did in order for him to skate," the Radfords reflect.

"We looked at each other and said, 'Well, we don't care if we travel all over the world during our retirement.'" They knew there would be a retirement pension from the teachers' union. "So you do what you think is the best for your child. That's what we've done all along."

The Radfords have since returned to live in Red Lake where Richard and their daughter-in-law Wendy are raising their family. Rick and Valerie reflect on what they do have, if not property. Eric competed at two Olympics, but for the Radfords, the fact that he went that far represents a truth they saw every time they watched him skate. He was developing, never regressing, even into the glittering twilight of his career.

Rick recalls a time when he took a few days off work in 2000 to drive to Winnipeg and watch Eric skate. Rick sat at the rink, striking up a conversation with another parent. "She didn't know me. She just made a comment, 'Oh, that Eric Radford. What a nice young man he is. And he's a good skater, too.'"

For the Radfords, that kind of comment means more than anything that could be written about Eric's skating. The skating community helps develop that personality, Rick adds.

"They're all very nice people. That's why Eric has turned out to be such a wonderful young man. He's hung out with great people," Rick says.

As for the fierce competitive gene, that comes from a pool of unknown origins. The Radford sons always wanted to be the best, the first, the one with the highest marks, the fastest out the school door for recess. "We don't have a clue how that happened. Our grandkids are the same," Rick says.

Valerie and Rick weren't really athletic as youngsters. Their era was simply different. Rick grew up on a farm in Central Ontario. There was no money for extracurricular sports when they were growing up, though Valerie did participate in some athletics through summer parks programming. She has worked since she was thirteen.

"I always wanted to do well in school. I worked hard and studied hard but Rick and I never had the opportunity to do anything in sports. So we made sure our boys had that opportunity. It didn't cost much to put our kids in sports in Balmertown and it was easy to take them to different things. Everything was so close."

Their sons were competitive in school and they always came home and talked about it. "They always wanted to do well. I guess I got lucky. Maybe it's expectations. I just wanted them to get out there and participate, to basically have fun and learn some skills."

They will always love how Eric moves on the ice. He was always musical, always had good programs. "And he was athletic. He learned how to do the jumps. Every coach he had told us he was very coachable," she adds.

They take heart in the way he coped with negativity throughout his career, a quality they see in Meagan, as well. They both stuck it out, through various partners, and Valerie recalls how when Eric and Meagan were first partnered, the skating world didn't appreciate the pairing.

"He's like a ballet dancer and she's very athletic," Valerie says. "They had a lot of negativity. But it never stopped them. I think that's the other part I like. Eric has never told me he's going to quit skating because somebody is saying this or somebody is saying that. Or because he couldn't find a skating partner," Valerie says.

In 2009 Eric and Rachel Kirkland parted ways after finishing seventh at Canadians. It was Eric's habit to talk to his parents every day, about virtually anything. Again they discussed his next move. He was twenty-four, and was working with Ingo. Eric talked of a possible move to Germany to train.

But the idea of Eric's moving to Germany was too much. Valerie has often felt she didn't know a lot about the inner workings of figure skating, but she knew enough to tell Eric he should call Skate Canada or talk to Richard Gauthier because he was coaching at a top pairs school in Montreal with Bruno Marcotte. Eric knew Bruno, having actually skated with him at one point in the tiny, one-degree-of-separation world of Canadian skating. Valerie flew in from Bermuda and talked to Richard about Eric's situation.

Clearly then it had been in the works that Bruno would be convincing Meagan that Eric should skate with her after her then partner Craig Buntin retired in 2010.

"You know what I said?" Valerie recalls, laughing. "'They'll never skate together. He's too tall. She's too short.' That's how much I know about skating. Richard told me they can do a triple Lutz. You watch.' "

Of all they discussed in the family van on the road and around the meal table, the Radfords had never really discussed retirement with Eric. Not even when he couldn't find a pairs partner, or when people teased him about being in a "girls' sport." Perhaps an injury might have forced that talk about leaving the sport; or the end of his partnership with Rachel in 2009, when Eric was at a crossroads. Financing the move to Germany and all that entailed was a daunting prospect for everyone. "It would have been very close to retirement, then," Rick adds. "But then Meagan came along."

Late in the summer of 2000, Meagan was wearing her parents down. Why can't she go to Barrie, and train at Mariposa Skating School that fall? Why, oh, why not? And on it went, for three weeks straight.

Today their daughter has a complete set of Olympic medals, is a two-time Olympian, a two-time world champion, and seven-time Canadian champion. But while much is blurry and forgotten, certain moments from a lifetime in figure skating still feel like yesterday. Heidi and Danny still wonder how they managed back when Meagan was starting out in the junior ranks: they worked two jobs each to keep the family afloat and Meagan's skating career alive, long before she was in the record books.

Meagan had come home from summer skating school in Barrie and more than once informed her parents that she wanted to move to Barrie to live, go to school and skate—not necessarily in that order. "It was a three-week struggle for us. She was so adamant. She cried, pleaded and begged every single day. It was really getting unnerving," Heidi and Danny recall.

"Meagan was going on and on, 'Why can't I go? I have to go.' And we're thinking, 'Oh my Lord, how could this ever work?'"

They told her they couldn't afford it and that she would have nowhere to live in Barrie. They reminded her she was only fourteen. School was about to start. Eventually they relented, saying she could stay for the first semester of school. Through a friend of the family, they found space with older roommates in a one-bedroom apartment, moved Meagan to Barrie, got her settled in, and left for home in Lively.

"We just dropped her off. How could we do that? We had to get home for work. We still had the other two kids at home. I remember driving home and there was a sense of relief." Everyone was happy knowing Meagan was happy in Barrie where she wanted to be. "You're not dropping off your child who's kicking and screaming because they'll have to stay there."

Still, they set the terms: she could come home any time if she didn't like skating in Barrie anymore or in general. If she regressed in the sport because she was fooling around, then she was definitely coming home. That fall, Meagan qualified for Canadians and stayed in Barrie. She would end up living in Barrie for the next seven years.

Meagan grew up in Lively, just west of Sudbury, nestled in the foothills of the La Cloche Mountain Range. Nowadays, Lively (one of the three towns that became "Walden" in the 1990s) is more of a bedroom community with a compact shopping district and new subdivisions, but prior to the amalgamation of Ontario municipalities by 2001, Walden was its own entity, with that fierce pride that comes from living next door to the big centre—in this case, Sudbury.

Among the claims to fame of ringette and hockey at the rink was the fact that in 1990, Walden Figure Skating Club member Jennifer Prouse won the novice ladies title on her home ice when Sudbury and Walden hosted the then Royal Bank Canadian Figure Skating Championships.

Meagan may have been too young to attend that event, but she lived on the corner of Turner and Irene in an older subdivision, well within walking distance of the arena and the outdoor ice pad.

And the apple didn't fall far from the Duhamel family tree.

While the Radfords didn't grow up with skating, the sport was part of the Duhamels' heritage. Heidi's grandfather had come from Finland to Timmins where skating was hugely popular in the 1960s. He told Heidi's parents that he'd roll over in his grave if they didn't put her in skating. He thought Heidi was too active and needed figure skating. Heidi's childhood friend, Kathy, skated with Ice Capades. Danny's sister, Rachael, skated at the Walden club. Danny and his brothers, Mike and Kevin, played local hockey. They all hung out at the outdoor rink down the road when their children were little.

In 1988, they were indoors at the local arena, watching the Walden Winter Carnival. Heather was five and Meagan was three. Heidi asked if they wanted to skate like that. The girls said, 'Yes!' Then at the end of every season Heidi would ask if the girls wanted to keep skating and the answer was always yes. They never complained when it was skating night, Heidi and Danny recall.

When Meagan was six, she would skate for an hour. After that session, Heather skated for two more hours. If it was Heidi's night to be the parent playing the music for the skaters, Meagan would join her mom in the music booth and watch the older skaters for those two hours. That's what she wanted to do. She didn't want to go home and play with her friends. Sometimes Meagan would bring her Barbies to the rink, but only to line them up on the boards to watch. Then she would go home and practise her sit spin on the ground. Or a Salchow.

"It seemed like the next skating day she would want to go out on the ice and do what she had seen the older girls doing. She was pretty much self-taught at that time," Heidi recalls.

Although they felt Meagan would absolutely require private skating lessons one day, she was the younger one, and Heather was already taking private skating lessons. Eventually, though, there was no putting off the lessons or the inevitable spring and summer schools in the local clubs in Greater Sudbury, and later east to North Bay. The Duhamels set up the trailer in nearby Sturgeon Falls and Heidi and Danny took turns with their respective two-week holidays so their daughters could skate at summer school for the entire month.

"We really never even thought about international competition, Worlds or Olympics. We didn't follow figure skating like that. It was just to make them better in what they were already competing in," Heidi and Danny say.

In the fall of 1998, Heather qualified for the 1999 Canadian Figure Skating Championships in the novice ladies division. Meagan, Danny and Heidi accompanied Heather to Canadians, and while Heather and her mother lived in a competition bubble, Danny sat with Meagan and watched every single event in every single division at Canadians that January.

It would be the pinnacle of Heather's career, that sixteenth place finish in Novice Ladies at Canadians, just behind Joannie Rochette. That following summer, Heather didn't skate in Barrie, but Meagan went and loved it so much she wanted to stay.

"That's when we figured out that this girl was so aware of what a national training centre was all about at such a young age that she must be serious about this," Danny and Heidi recall. "Even hearing coach Doug Leigh telling her if she landed her triple flip, which was the last of her triple jumps that she needed to land, then she could move up to the elite session. That was pretty impressive to hear, coming from him. He had coached Elvis Stojko.

"She was so aware of what this was all about, more than we were. All the way through her career, she has educated us. We didn't even know half of what was involved and all the demands that needed to be met."

Although the Duhamels mostly parented Meagan over the phone, they were also close enough, in relative Northern Ontario terms, to drive the three hundred kilometres south to Barrie. Heidi would watch Meagan practise, then bring her home for the weekend, before driving back to Barrie on Sunday to drop her off, and then return home. Other family members and friends also chipped in with riders to and from Barrie.

On the weekends when she came home, Meagan would lie in bed and read autobiographies of different figure skaters to her mother. "That was our little thing. Once she asked what I would say when they interview me some day," Heidi says.

After six months in Barrie in 2000, Megan had qualified to skate as a junior at Canadians, and then there was no point bringing her back to Lively. Her living conditions eventually improved but the family will only say that her first apartment was less than ideal. "We only learned years later that Meagan had often cried herself to sleep," Heidi recalls.

She speaks in a mellow tone as she recounts those times but there is also a hint in here that there would have been no arguing if Danny and Heidi had known exactly what was going on. "She knew we would bring her back home in a heartbeat if we ever found out."

Boarding was perhaps the hardest aspect of having Meagan away for skating. They wanted her to live in a home where she would be treated as part of the family. That didn't happen until Meagan was able to drive. Then she moved in with extended family south of Barrie, in Bradford. "This move ended up being the best blessing for us and Meagan."

Meagan was skating singles and pairs with Ryan Arnold while working part-time to pay for gas and to have extra spending money, but Heidi and Danny also added part-time jobs to their full-time work to keep everyone afloat. Heidi worked days at the Sudbury hospital, and then the night shift at a local retirement home.

Danny quit his men's hockey league to referee in winter. He officiated baseball games in the summer and stayed home with their son Johnny while Heidi worked until midnight. Heather was in university and Heidi wrote letters to help their eldest child secure bursaries. Heather also worked part-time. Johnny played rep hockey and lacrosse, delivered newspapers, and cut grass to earn extra spending money.

Still, the accounts didn't always balance. Cheques often were returned NSF. Cheques to Meagan's coach were mailed back. "My heart would skip a beat. It was so embarrassing, calling the coach and saying, 'Your cheque is not going to go through.' Bless his soul for he seemed to be so understanding," Heidi recalls.

In 2005, Danny lost his job and Meagan had to forgo costly private lessons for a time. "We had more money going out than coming in," Heidi and Danny say. So they looked for local sponsors. Lively is a funny borough, however. Meagan was beginning to achieve success yet even token sponsorship was hard to come by. Requests were ignored, usually.

But Heidi and Danny prefer to remember that there were those who did step up. In 2003, loaded with her bills from Mariposa, Heidi sat across from the owner of a local fuel company and began to cry as she made the request for sponsorship. He asked for the total and paid the $5,000 tab. "I cannot say how low I felt that I had to bring myself to plead to a complete stranger for financial support. Somebody please, this girl is going to be good someday."

But coupled with the need to pay for everything was another fear. Heidi and Danny wondered about receiving sponsorship only to have Meagan promptly decide to retire. "And here we'd taken money from people, so that was our dilemma as well."

The Duhamels even wondered if Meagan was really going to reach the upper levels in the sport of figure skating. Meagan was identified at a talent development camp in the Northern region. Later, Heidi called the judge and asked point-blank if Meagan really had talent. "You know, everybody thinks their child is good. When people would comment about Meagan's talent, I still wasn't sure. I'm not really that gullible."

Chip Duncan, a local judge who often came to watch the skating in Walden, stood beside Heidi at the boards one night. Watching Meagan, he said, "That kid is Worlds material."

They found ways to stick it out and even follow Meagan's path. Greyhound offered a companion-rides-for-free deal, so in January of 2004, they rode the bus to Edmonton to watch Meagan, the only Northern Ontario skater, compete and finish tenth in senior ladies at Canadians. They were laughing when they stopped in Blind River, a two-hour drive west of Lively. "We've got thirty hours left to go. Two hours down, thirty to go."

The weather in January was, naturally, way below freezing. For whatever reason—it's all a blur now—they were stuck in Winnipeg, Manitoba, on the trip west and the bus wasn't leaving until the next morning.

They hadn't invested in luggage even though they often travelled to watch Meagan compete. Heidi was superstitious: she believed that the moment they bought suitcases, Meagan would end her skating career. "I never took for granted that she would keep skating this long," Heidi adds.

That night in Winnipeg, Heidi and Danny pondered whether they had enough money to stay in a hotel or if they would have to sleep at the bus station. They sprang for the hotel, opened their duffel bags full of frozen clothes and began thawing the blocks of ice. Clothes were scattered all over the hotel room.

Now they fly, with luggage, and sometimes Meagan springing for the tickets. They jetted to Japan, Regina and Vancouver in the months before the 2018 Olympics. The financial struggles and three years of working two jobs each are now so long ago. Their dedication created an opportunity for Meagan which she never took for granted, Danny and Heidi add.

"We look back and we have no idea how we came through without losing our house, without losing a little bit of our dignity, and while trying to make sure our other two children at home always felt we were there for them and that we loved our children equally."

Heidi and Danny always appreciated Meagan's love and boundless enthusiasm for the sport, and the strides she and Eric made in pairs figure skating.

They view the Olympics and the other world skating events as a bonus on top of the massive cake of Meagan's career. In the end, they remain amazed at Meagan's persistence and resilience, despite the setbacks, the barriers and the issues that arose in her health and living conditions.

"She went to Mariposa and treated skating as her job. She gave it her all. It is such a judged sport. You're fighting against the odds. You have to wait sometimes and earn your stripes," Heidi and Danny reflect.

And some things never change. A younger Meagan would be practising and then she'd skate over, tap on the window and ask, "Did you see me, did you see me? That was a single." Later it was three fingers, a triple jump. Later it was four fingers, and Meagan asking, "Did you see my quad?"

"That's what we love about her: she's just so passionate in every aspect, as a fan and as a competitor herself. We're so happy she found a partner like Eric. It was fate that the two from Northern Ontario ended up skating together, making each other's dreams a reality."

Meagan Duhamel and Eric Radford with Laura E. Young

THE EARLY YEARS:
LET THE PASSION BEGIN

Eric: Skater, Skier, Piano Player

Eric may not entirely remember the seven-year-old his parents describe, jumping and spinning in the living room as he watched figure skating on TV. What remains vivid is how Nancy Kerrigan led him to skating. The American skater famously won the 1994 Olympic silver medal. Eric recalls her 1992 bronze medal, however, and a series of stars.

"It looked like flying to me. At the very end of her program Nancy did what we call stars, a moving camel spin across the ice. It looked like so much fun. The way she moved with the music, something clicked in my brain: I wanted to learn to do that. I also watched Kurt Browning and Elvis Stojko all the time. But to skate like Nancy, that's what I wanted.

"I also curled, swam and did all the school sports competitively, as well as gymnastics and cross-country skiing. I did a different sport every day and I was skating three times a week—Tuesdays, Thursdays, and Saturdays, for two hours. We did patch, free skate, and dance at that time.

"I was fairly serious about gymnastics and trained with the club in Balmertown. My best tumbling pass was a round-off back handspring, back whipback, back handspring, back tuck. I could also do a back pike. My goal in gymnastics was to learn a full twisting layout on the floor. That's all I ever wanted to do. I was starting to work on the full twist but just as I was about to learn it, I landed wrong and felt my left ankle go. I had a hairline fracture which took me out of everything for quite a while."

After the accident, Eric continued in gymnastics for another two years. He would make the big trek south to Thunder Bay for summer camp, starting at the age of nine. His first year, he could do all the tumbling and was one of the better gymnasts. But every year following his first, he noticed the other kids had not only caught up to him, they were surpassing him. He seemed to have reached a plateau. He realized he didn't want to move away from home and pursue gymnastics—he was as good as he was going to be.

Figure skating was beckoning now, and he couldn't ignore its call. By the end of Grade 8, also his final year in gymnastics, Eric had started to grow and he knew he would be too tall and too lean for the sport of compact, muscular athletes. But in skating, he was landing his double jumps and had finished second at the provincial championships.

Besides, he loved skating, and even three days of skating a week was not enough. He always looked forward to it, even though the bullying was relentless. He was the only boy skating in Red Lake. The only other boy at the rink drove from Ear Falls every other weekend to skate.

As Eric and his parents recount his early years, Eric makes it clear that although they can laugh about it all now, at the time it wasn't funny at all. Grade 8 was one of the worst years he endured. He was bullied with the double wallop of sexism and homophobia: he was in figure skating and gymnastics, two so-called girls' sports.

"I was teased at school. I still remember a girl asking me why my parents treat me like a girl. When I asked her what she meant, she said, 'They put you in gymnastics and they put you in figure skating and those are girls' sports.' I told her that they didn't put me in, that I wanted to do those sports.

"But that was just a small-town mentality at that time. I think it's changed a lot. There were times when the teasing discouraged me. When I won competitions, there would be articles in the local newspaper about me. Then the teasing would lessen, but it never stopped.

Kids yelled names and often tripped Eric up as he walked down the hallway. Outside of school he tried to avoid everybody. They would yell names at him across the street if they saw him. Once, a large group of his tormentors waited for him outside the rink. He walked through them. It was terrifying and humiliating, he says.

"But the girls who I skated with at the rink were supportive. They would tell me not to listen. 'One day you're going to be on TV and they're going to be at home with a beer in their hand watching you.' And, eventually, it all happened. But that last year in Balmertown was really tough.

"When I made the decision to move away for Grade 9, I thought that I had to make the most of it. I really almost recreated myself. I don't even know if my mom even noticed but in Grade 8 I used to speak with a lisp. Over the summer I taught myself how to speak without it. Kids would make fun of me all the time. They said I sounded gay.

"Richard would sit with me and show me how to keep my tongue inside my lower teeth and sound out things. Slowly, the lisp went away. My mom never said anything about it. We would be sitting in the van driving somewhere and I'd be looking in the mirror watching my mouth make the shapes while my brother told me how to speak.

"I really was just the biggest nerd. I loved doing well at school but that wasn't cool. You're supposed to not care. I played piano for at least an hour a day and I loved it. I always wanted to be the best; I wanted to be the fastest. I wanted to be the first in line. I wanted to get the highest marks. I was such an easy target, especially in a small town."

Valerie was very organized with her sons' activities and it helped that Eric loved doing all of his sports, and had a seemingly endless store of energy. On weekend mornings his friends would invite him tobogganing, and although he experienced momentary disappointment when his mother reminded him he had a skiing lesson, as soon as he was on the ski trails he forgot his disappointment.

When Eric looks back at the early videos of his skating, he sees a skater who was a little uncoordinated until he was fifteen or sixteen. His talent lay in learning through watching, imagining and feeling. That may well be his secret to excelling in most sports.

Early on, though, skating emerged as the sport Eric seemed destined to follow. At barely thirteen years old, he landed his very first triple. When he started training with Paul Wirtz at age fifteen, Eric became a jumper.

"I can still remember to this day, that it was April 14, 2001, when I landed all of my triple jumps cleanly on one day. Paul helped me get all those jumps. My whole skating career changed that year because he turned me into a really good jumper. He also told me to own my classical style. I had never thought about my body or the way I skated. He told me I was going to be a classical skater, so be that.

"I think Paul's original intention when I started skating with him was for me to be a pairs skater. I was tall. He used to have me do lifts with the girls off-ice. But then when I started to get all my triple jumps, he thought that maybe I would have some sort of career in singles and allowed me to pursue that more. It wasn't until 2003 that I started skating with Sarah Burke.

"In pairs it's not so much about height. It's about your stature. If you're really tall and lanky it's going to be difficult because you don't have as much strength. The longer your limb is, the more strength it takes to lift. Olympic weightlifters aren't six feet tall, they're short and strong.

"Height has its advantages and disadvantages. The taller you are, the more power you need to have in order to generate the force to lift. At the same time, because I'm tall, I can have nice lines on the ice and lifts can look nice.

"It's different for everybody when they decide to become a pairs skater. Some coaches have the philosophy that you should decide as soon as possible so you learn the pairs skills right away. One of the best pieces of advice I ever received came from Dennis Silverthorne. I used to go to summer school in London where he taught. He was an older coach who flew airplanes in World War Two. He said learn to skate first, then you can learn to skate with somebody else. When I look at how everything happened with my and Meagan's career, that's exactly the advice that we followed."

Moving away from home to skate was a big, scary change but for the most part Eric lucked out. He boarded with great families. In Kenora, his first family had two daughters and an older son, who had just left for university. Eric took his room in the basement.

"My mom had forgotten to tell them that sometimes I get night terrors. One time I woke up screaming and didn't know where I was. I remember hearing a knock at my door, waking up and going over, opening it up and they were both standing there with baseball bats. I was like, 'Is everything okay? Are you okay? Yeah, I'm fine.' But I remembered it like a dream.

"The next morning they told me that they had thought somebody was killing me. When they heard my blood-curdling screams they thought I was being stabbed. They had come downstairs and I had locked my door and they couldn't get in."

Rosie called Valerie and admitted she wasn't sure Eric could stay there anymore; that she had never thought about what would happen if something happened to Eric. Valerie said, "Oh. I forgot to tell you about his night terrors."

Valerie and Rick parented Eric over the phone. He left when he was thirteen and lived a year in Kenora, then a year in Winnipeg and one year in Montreal. Eric would get so homesick. There would be nights he would just cry. He'd talk to Valerie on the phone for an hour. She would remind him that he could always come home. Eric never broke enough. He would just say, "No, I don't need to come home. I just need to talk to you."

And, as always, there was the piano. Piano was something he could do at home, after skating, wherever he was living. In Kenora he lived in two different homes where they both happened to have pianos. When he moved to Winnipeg, he brought his electronic keyboard along.

"Piano was something that I loved to do. My piano was always there for me whenever I was homesick, or whenever I had a bad day at skating or at school. I could lose myself in piano. And it's still like that."

During his first year in Kenora, Eric had two music teachers who instilled a confidence in the skater, and showed him that he could also consider pursuing music seriously. Wherever he lived, Valerie found a piano teacher for him, usually one within a bus ride from his billet or school. When he moved to Montreal, at fifteen, his piano teacher would come to his house.

"I honestly can't think of anything that would have sent me home unless my parents ran out of money or I had an injury. I'd already survived the bullying. I don't know if going home after that would have made it worse. I think that going away, then coming back wouldn't have been as bad as staying. Going away gave you a certain cachet. You went away and you did something. My brother went on an exchange and after he came back, people thought it was really cool that he had spent a year living in Australia.

"I had changed myself in those years, as well. I remember hearing a speech by the actor Wentworth Miller who had come out as gay. He said he had to be so aware of all his mannerisms when he was growing up, or people would have made fun of him. I didn't realize it then, but I was the same way. I remember being aware of, and in control of, how I spoke and how I carried myself."

Despite the bullying and taunting, Eric possessed a certain natural grit and directed his gaze toward a broader horizon. When he was twelve, just before he moved away, he would walk down the street in Red Lake and even though he was outdoors he would feel claustrophobic. He identified with Ariel in the Little Mermaid, possessing a conviction that there had to be so much more than this small town. He had a yearning inside, even at a young age, to live his life in the larger world, not just in a town, a city or even a country. He wanted a global life.

It all happened—on quite a scale. But it wouldn't come in singles skating. The 2005 sectionals event that October was his last event in singles. He was officially a pairs skater.

Meagan: Gymnast, Tennis Player, Figure Skater

It's appropriate that Meagan's early days of performance, and the joy that performing still brings her today, began with her connection to Up with People, the international youth troupe that travels the globe for six months of every year volunteering and performing. Her cousin Christina Koski toured the world with Up with People. She would choreograph routines for Meagan, who adored dancing with her.

And, like Eric, Meagan played every sport she could: T-ball, tennis, swimming, skating. When Heather suffered a concussion in gymnastics, their mother pulled them out. But skating remained on the fridge calendar. Every September when it was time for skating registration Heidi would ask, "Do you want to do skating lessons again or not?" Meagan always said yes.

Eventually it came down to dance lessons and skating lessons. Meagan was either going to skate four nights a week or go to dance.

"There was something fascinating about skating to me. It combined performance with sport. As a kid I liked any type of a show that included music and performing, people dressing up as animals or any characters. I never liked cartoon characters or animated stuff. I liked real live performance with music, singing, and dancing.

"I liked the challenge of trying to learn something new, a new jump, a new spin. What's the next thing to learn? What can I achieve next? It's an endless list in skating. My sister also skated which was a big plus for me. I was like any young kid who just wants to do what their older sibling does.

"Ever since I can remember I've been hooked on skating. I just wanted to skate all the time even if I was sick. If I didn't want to go to school on a given day, I'd pretend to be sick. But my mom said, 'If you don't go to school, you can't go skating tonight,' so I always changed my mind and told her I'd go. I didn't want to miss my skating lesson."

When Meagan began competing she often finished at the bottom of the pile, but she was still qualifying out of the Northern Ontario skating division to compete against skaters from across the rest of Ontario, and then Canada. She was improving.

In January of 1999 Heather qualified for Canadians. Skate Canada would hold a pairs tryout after nationals. All the novice and junior teams used to break up after nationals if they weren't going to continue, so there would be an open tryout to make new pairs teams. Meagan's coach got wind of it and told her to try it, that it would be fun for Meagan to do.

Meagan went to this tryout by herself. There were only four male skaters and what seemed like one hundred female skaters. In fact, Craig Buntin, her future partner, was one of the guys there.

"I was so shy. I would skate in circles, do my double Axel and go back to the boards. We had to wait for a guy to ask one of us to skate with him. I didn't know what to do. Everyone else had coaches with them. Mine wasn't. My mom was ready to take me off the ice if I didn't start skating. Louis Stong, who was then working for Skate Canada, took my hand and told me to ask those boys to skate with me or get off the ice. I was so scared. I didn't know what to do. Eventually some of the boys asked me to skate."

After the tryout, Meagan went home and Lee Barkell, a coach in Barrie, contacted her coach and asked Meagan to come for another tryout in March. Tiny and dynamic and packing a double Axel jump, Meagan had attracted someone's attention. She went to Barrie with Heidi for the trial. Meagan relished the experience and enjoyed learning all sorts of new things and playing around on the ice. She and Heidi met with Lee and discussed Meagan's skating. But moving away from home at twelve was a little extreme.

It was Meagan's first exposure to a training centre. Elvis Stojko, one of her skating heroes, was still skating there. But she was young and after returning home, soon forgot the experience. She didn't consider skating competitively beyond junior ladies.

In 2000 Heidi registered fourteen-year-old Meagan for the four-week summer skating camp at Mariposa. A lot of the kids she was skating with in her age group started talking about moving to Barrie to live and skate at Mariposa full time. Meagan didn't know that was possible, but once she did, the campaign began. A lot of the skaters there had Team Canada jackets, and were going to the Olympics and World Championships. Meagan was insistent that she needed to be in Barrie if she wanted to do the same.

She told her parents that she needed to stay in Barrie for the rest of the summer. It was expensive so her parents brought her home. Meagan skated in summer school in Sudbury for the next month, but she didn't let Mariposa go. With unwavering, even unnerving insistence, Meagan kept pestering her parents that she needed to move to Barrie.

Heather had no desire to go back to Barrie but Meagan didn't want to come home. Her eyes had been opened to something. That August, she competed at Skate Ontario Summer Skate in Thornhill where she landed a triple Salchow and a double Axel en route to winning novice ladies. It was a big deal to win a competition outside of Northern Ontario. Meagan was starting to achieve good results. She needed to go to Barrie, to be with the best. She learned about the ISU (International Skating Union) Junior Grand Prix and said that's what she needed to do.

"Eventually, through begging and being a brat, and crying and whatever else convinced my parents to let me go, I went. I was supposed to be there for one semester of high school. But at the end of that semester I qualified for my first Nationals, which were held in the second semester, in January. One semester turned into a year, then turned into two years, and then seven years later I was still there.

"I was torn between two worlds. I was forced to grow up quickly when I was fourteen. I didn't live in the best places: I would say that I lived with interesting people. I was living with two adults and sleeping on their couch in their one-bedroom apartment. They weren't from the same family structure I was and they weren't really around much. I didn't even know how to boil water. I would call my mom, and she would tell me over the phone how to make Kraft Dinner. Every few months I was moving and living in a different house. I was never homesick enough to go home. I realized that this was what I needed to do if I wanted to go to the Olympics."

In the early days in Barrie, Meagan relied on rides with people or just walked everywhere. Walking was easy. She lived down the street from the rink. The school and the rink shared the same parking lot.

"Except, I wasn't exactly going to school all the time. I was skipping classes so I could skate more. The school didn't have a parent to call because I didn't have parents in Barrie, so I could get away with that. The rink would write me notes: 'She was skating, that's why she missed class.' Then the school year was over and I'd have ninety missed days and I'd be failing my classes.

"But there were so many kids my age living away from home at this time. We were alone but we weren't alone because we had each other. Some kids had a parent there; their moms moved or their whole families moved, which happened a lot."

Jennifer Robinson was skating in Mariposa then. She was the top Canadian ladies skater for many years. Meagan loved to train with her. Jennifer was so diligent, so hard-working, Meagan recalls. When Jennifer made the 2002 Olympic team, Meagan and her friend Erica bought Jennifer a skating book and the Olympic Barbie and wrote her a letter about how inspiring she was because she was going to the Olympics. That was such an unforeseen experience for Meagan, that she was actually training with people who were going to the Salt Lake City Olympics.

"My results were often frustrating. I was up and down like a yo-yo as a singles skater. I could win a competition, and then I would be eighth. Every season would end and I would reassess. What do I need to do to be better? What am I missing? It was this constant evolution of what else do I need to do. I was so hungry to go to the Olympics and be like Jennifer Robinson, so I was always searching for the next best thing.

"In 2004 my friend Ryan Arnold was looking for a pairs partner. We started playing around in practice and within five minutes I had landed a throw triple Lutz.

"Ryan said, 'Whoa, wait a second. You shouldn't be able to do that so easily.' We showed our coach and he asked us if we wanted to skate pairs as well as skate singles. Of course I wanted to. I thought I could win at both and skate at Worlds and the Olympics in pairs and singles. I was so ambitious."

Pairs started as a fluke for Meagan, but from the outset, Ryan and Meagan could easily do a few elements that were very impressive. Now Meagan was training pairs and singles equally, which was a lot of skating: two hours of pairs, two hours of singles each day. It was also expensive. She ended up working at Staples Business Depot part time to help cover her expenses.

Meagan was enjoying success in both disciplines. She qualified for the national team in singles. Ryan and Meagan finished second in Nebelhorn Trophy in Germany. At Canadians in 2005, Meagan finished seventh in singles and she and Ryan were eighth in pairs. In 2006 she was fourth in singles and sixth in pairs.

"I really liked skating in singles because I could only rely on and control myself. I could work hard at the pace I wanted to work at. I didn't have to rely on somebody else to do anything for me. I liked that. I liked having control over my entire career."

Money remained a challenge. After the 2006 Canadians there was little to go around. Meagan didn't have much and at this point Heidi and Danny were no longer able to help finance her skating career. Meagan felt like she was standing at a crossroads. She needed to make a decision. She opted to continue in singles—it made the most sense. She was getting a bit of funding because her placing in singles was high at the national and international levels. She had just gone to Four Continents and finished fifth, which was a good result for her, and she was going to receive Grand Prix assignments the following year as a singles skater. She could envision her career going down that road.

Although pairs skating was fun, Meagan was convinced that she had made the right decision to remain a singles skater. Then, a year later, she changed her mind. She had two stress fractures in her left foot. She had received assignments to skate in Grand Prix events in singles in the fall of 2006, but the injuries kept her home. She missed a good portion of that season. After getting back on the ice that fall, she was skating at Mariposa when she collided with Patrick Chan, who was training there for a few days. Meagan hurt her knee and had to sit out skating for another week or two.

When Meagan came back, she collided with another skater. Meagan was performing a spiral and the other skater was attempting a flying camel spin when they ran into each other. Meagan needed stitches in her shoulder, deep into the muscle. The scar is still there. After recovering from her shoulder injury, she developed shingles. Now she was starting to question her future in the sport. All these obstacles had prevented Meagan from improving, and she never wanted to remain stagnant. She was always searching for ways to push for more. "That was a helluva year," she remarks.

"When the season finished in January 2007 I started thinking about what else I needed to do in order to make it onto the podium at Canadians. I thought of changing coaches. I thought of getting new choreographers. I thought of moving somewhere else. I never thought it would be my last year as a singles skater. I was in this wishy-washy area when I got the phone call from Craig Buntin in Montreal."

2010–2014: OUR FIRST OLYMPIC CYCLE

In any post-Olympic shuffle, the excitement and sense of change in figure skating can rival the NHL and the NBA at the trade deadline. Who can we get to take us to the next level? Who is undiscovered and not reaching their full potential? What combinations will create the magic?

Meagan had considered other pair partners, if she ultimately decided to keep skating. Perhaps Dylan Moscovitch? His pairing with Kirsten Moore-Towers was only one year old. They were doing well together but maybe he would want to try out with Meagan?

Bruno Marcotte, her pairs coach, disagreed and told her she would be trying out with Eric Radford. And Meagan disagreed. She could picture herself skating with Dylan, who is also athletic and powerful and seemed like a better match to Meagan's skating. Again, Bruno insisted on Eric.

Eric and Meagan had known each other since they were little. Eric had seen Meagan and Heather's names on the results sheet during events in the Northern Ontario Section. He recalls thinking it was so interesting that two sisters were such good skaters. Later, Meagan and Eric had travelled together as singles skaters to compete in their first international assignments in Chicago and Slovenia. They had competed against each other with their previous partners at home and abroad. They were neighbours and good friends. But they had never considered skating together.

Back in Canada, it was nearly midnight in early February 2010 and subterfuge was crackling in the winter air. Marcotte, coach Richard Gauthier, and Eric and Meagan convened in Patinoire CCJJS Arena on Montreal's south shore. Eric had a sense of the clandestine as he drove from the Island of Montreal south to Sainte-Julie. It was such a bizarre time to skate. The only ice available was in the smallest of the three rinks in the complex.

Meagan had partied hard in Korea and was out of shape—by her high standards. Then there was the matter of commitments: she and Craig had shows to perform in, as did Eric and Anne-Marie. Then Craig would retire. Aside from the fear of failure and pain in skating, Meagan was insistent that Eric already had a partner in Anne-Marie. Her coaches were equally adamant, saying, 'If you and Eric aren't good together, why would Eric break up with Anne-Marie to skate with you? There's nobody else for him. If he breaks up with her, tries out with you and it's terrible, he's stuck without a partner.'

"Our coaches told me that Eric shouldn't break up with Anne-Marie until we knew whether we would skate together. If Eric didn't skate with me, he had no other choice but to continue with Anne-Marie. That is why Eric did our tryout behind Anne-Marie's back.

"We could only get ice time at midnight, which is partly why it was so terrible. I wasn't really serious. The first time we skated together our tracking was so off. We couldn't find each other. I'm watching him, he's watching me. We were grabbing and yanking on each other to try and set our timing.

"I've seen a lot of tryouts. It takes five minutes. They skate around the rink and you're like, 'Oh, that looks so good.' That was not Eric and me. Our timing was terrible. Eric couldn't lift me. He said, 'I don't get it. You're so small and I'm so big.' "

Eric wondered what the coaches were thinking when they matched him with Meagan. When he first lifted Meagan that night he thought it shouldn't be so difficult. He reflects how Meagan was shorter than his other partners, but she felt heavier because of the lack of technique and timing. Because Craig had been shorter than Eric, Meagan would get into position right away before she was above Eric's head. As soon as Meagan stopped her momentum, Eric's momentum stopped. He couldn't even lift Meagan above his head.

Craig was six inches shorter than Eric, so Meagan wasn't used to waiting so long to get to the top of the lift. The timing on Meagan and Eric's jumps was different and so they struggled to even do a double Axel side by side, says Eric.

"My initial reservation was just our style—our bodies and our styles mismatching artistically. We were going to be able to do very well technically, but when you get to the point where you're among the top five teams in the world, they all do the technical things and the same elements. The second mark makes the difference.

"But I think that right from the beginning Meagan was saying, 'I'll do whatever it takes.' I had never skated with somebody like that before. I'm going to do whatever it takes and she's going to do whatever it takes. We both wanted the same thing, so what was there to prevent us from achieving what we want to, other than ourselves?"

Richard asked them to try a triple Lutz side by side. Meagan hadn't tried that jump in four years. The jump was terrible, but she wasn't upset because she had no expectations going into the tryout.

Richard's concern was that people would see Eric and Meagan as two different skaters, not a pair. Bruno was more adamant that it would work. He kept saying, 'No, Isabelle and Lloyd were the same with a big height difference and people didn't mind. It's going to be okay.' Bruno sold it to Richard and in turn they sold the idea of the pairing of Eric and Meagan to Eric and Meagan.

Years later, from the home he and Meagan share, Bruno hustles their dogs out of the room and continues explaining why he was so convinced the pair would work. Yes, their tryout was rough and the pair elements were tough to watch, but he just had this feeling.

"They always felt that if you want to succeed at something, you need something that will put you ahead. That will get you noticed. The things that they missed in the tryout for me were just about getting used to their height difference. But I really believed they had the same passion for the sport. They both came from Northern Ontario. They were singles skating champions. They had a lot of things in common. They also had the same goals. Eric had skated with some really good partners, but no one could really match Eric's ability to jump, until Meagan was paired with him."

And, it had been heartbreaking when Meagan and Craig just missed a spot on the Olympic team. "But I knew Meagan still had the passion for the sport. I knew that she felt that she didn't accomplish as much as she wanted. Mainly it's not always about winning the gold medal but it's to finish on your own terms as far as giving it your all and finishing with a good positive experience.

"I knew they were going to work so hard. Their friendship was going to allow them to eventually reach their goals. That's why I never had a doubt that it would work."

Meagan and Eric looked at Bruno like he had three heads. Meagan went home to figure out her future. Eric left for vacation in Australia, but first he had a meeting with Anne-Marie, his current partner, to end the pairing. It was difficult to say the least, Eric remembers.

"Then we finally sat down and had a meeting with Anne-Marie and her dad and said this is what's happening. It was really hard. It was the second time I'd had to do it. When I split with Rachel it was really difficult as well. It's not a nice feeling breaking up with somebody. Obviously, it was the right decision.

"I think for me it was based on my own singles skating ability. I could do all my triples. I was pretty good at most of the pairs skills. I was a consistent skater.

"Sometimes you see a skater and you say, 'Oh, she could be a really good pairs skater. You see a small little pre-novice but then you see them jump and they don't quite have a double Axel yet and you can't really tell if it's going to happen.

"But I wasn't waiting for a jump, I wasn't waiting for the ability to do something. It was already there. I just needed the opportunity to show it."

Meagan acknowledges she did not have the best working relationship with Craig, but she never worried about that with Eric. They may have disagreed from time to time, but they were never so frustrated with the other that they couldn't work through things as a team with a common goal. Their mutual Northern Ontario roots were merely a happy

Meagan Duhamel and Eric Radford with Laura E. Young

coincidence for the two friends but they did know instinctively what it was like to drive and drive, sometimes through blinding snowstorms, where being behind a transport truck is actually helpful. They knew what their parents had sacrificed so they could afford to skate.

There were doubts across the board, perhaps even some exhaustion in both families. Still, Heidi Duhamel recalls a quiet, seemingly random moment between the two skaters in 2009 when Eric and Meagan were in Montreal training together but with different partners. At the end of one particularly rough day, Eric quietly passed Meagan a note. It read: "Tomorrow will be a better day."

Bruno laughs at the suggestion that he and Richard Gauthier looked like brilliant masterminds for having paired Meagan and Eric. They didn't put a timeline or a deadline on Meagan and Eric. But once Eric and Meagan started skating together they gelled quickly. Right from the beginning, they were such analysis freaks, knowing every micro value of every element, he says.

They launched a four-year plan to compete at the 2014 Winter Olympics in Sochi, Russia. "Usually when skaters get to a certain age and they reach the senior level it becomes more or less a four-year project. After that you reassess if you want to get yourself into the commitment of another four years," Bruno says.

"And what's impressive about them is every year they took some goals and they were able to reach those goals. The first year they came seventh at Worlds. The next year they came fifth. Then the next year the goal was to be top three. They reached that. They were able to have a fast rise to the top."

He and Julie Marcotte, their choreographer, would often predict how their skaters would do. Bruno said that they had to land all their jumps, which meant they had to skate cleanly, otherwise, they would suffer at the hands of the judges. The pair team would be introduced to the world through their jumps, and their ability as singles skaters.

It was a risky strategy; however, without that certain "je ne sais quoi", a something, Bruno says that Meagan and Eric would have never had a shot at becoming world champions. They would rise to the top with the side-by-side triple Lutz jump.

They could not play it safe either, or Bruno thought they'd always finish fifth or even seventh in the world. He told them that if they wanted to be on the podium, it would be through the side-by-side triple Lutz, and they would be the only team in the world to do it.

For Bruno there was hope in the new pair and belief in their mission, but at the end of the day, Eric and Meagan made it happen, he says. "They were never satisfied, not once, with their skating or their placement. They appreciated what they had accomplished but then they would say, 'Okay, what's the next step?' "

And so, in the spring of 2010, an unlikely team started training together, turning, perhaps even risking, a friendship into an on-ice partnership. Meagan had recently recovered from her accumulated injuries, and Eric was just back from Australia.

On the ice, they were just another pair of athletes in the busy mix and mingle of gloved and yoga gear-clad skaters working in the fresh spring of a Montreal morning.

Then as Eric loves to recall, he threw Meagan for the first time.

"With my two previous partners, throws were always a risky element for us. The first throw triple Salchow we did, Meagan landed it so easily. It wasn't just that she hung on, it was a really nice throw triple Salchow. That was the very beginning of seeing our potential. The probability of achieving what I thought I could do just skyrocketed.

"I was so happy I almost cried. It's just such a feeling of 'We're really good, wow.' It was a whole new game for me. In the first week, it was as if this whole new door had opened. All of a sudden the dream of going to the Olympics and the dream of being a competitor on the world stage became a possibility and a reality again. Until then I didn't know what this sport held for me, if it held anything. I didn't know if I was going to stay in it for much longer."

By the end of the week Eric and Meagan could do two side-by-side triple jumps, and throw triple jumps, and they could skate clean run-throughs with those elements. It was something Eric had never really been able to do before. It completely changed his entire outlook.

"I had started to believe that I was bad at doing throws. There are different ways of seeing the throw and your role in it. I know in Russia, it's the guy's fault if the girl misses. But part of Meagan's talent at skating is just being able to land anything. She's always been known to be cat-like, that way."

Meagan could do so much of it by herself. It seemed like she could do a throw triple Salchow with any partner. Eric recalls a story where Meagan was auditioning for a commercial with Joey Russell, who was a singles skater at the time. They did a throw triple Salchow. Joey understood the mechanics of the element but Meagan was really, really good at landing that, as Eric says.

"But it wasn't just the throw Salchow. We did the throw loop and the throw Lutz that week as well. We did all the hard triples in the first week. All I could think was, 'Wow, that was really impressive.'

"I think part of our strength, especially in the beginning, is that we were on the same page so naturally. We finished each other's sentences. We liked the same type of music. We used to hang out every night and it was this crazy amazing adventure in the beginning."

Bruno had quietened their initial objections by saying give it a week. It they couldn't do it comfortably that week, they didn't have to skate together. It didn't take them long, maybe ten hours of practice and they could skate level-four triple jumps, among other key pair elements, Meagan recalls. "Even if our bodies didn't match, we were usually synchronized. Eric is able to watch and track so that we were always able to step on the same foot at the same time. I can't focus on that type of stuff. Like, learning how to spin. Eric was able to just watch and be exactly where he needed to be. Eric was strikingly different from my previous partner that way.

"That was a big thing: I didn't have to look for Eric because he was always putting himself where he needed to be. He's extremely consistent. There were days where we couldn't do something, but there weren't long stretches of time where Eric would be up and down like a yo-yo."

From a technical standpoint, they were quick to learn all the jumps, throws and twists. The level four elements came easily. They skipped the normal phases of learning as they progressed through the levels—they mastered level four death spirals and spins right away.

Bruno told them that if they wanted to go to Worlds, there would be no favours. And that was true. Every time they skated clean they were rewarded and every time there was a mistake they were taken down. If they didn't skate cleanly, they would pay. The judges wouldn't help because the second mark, for component scores, was still behind their technical marks.

They took to adding to their already strong technical repertoire, too. Meagan recalls that at Christmas, just mid-way through the season, they learned a throw triple twist. There was no ice available so they headed to a tiny rink in Saint-Leonard. The walls were right at the boards of the ice.

"I had played around with the triple twist with my first partner, Ryan, but we had never done it consistently. Throws were so natural to me because they simulated my own jumping style. When I learned a throw triple Lutz, it was simulating my own triple Lutz as a singles skater. But a triple twist didn't simulate anything I already knew.

"When I first learned to skate pairs, it took a ridiculously long eight weeks to learn a single twist. Back when I was skating with Ryan, the twist and the pairs spin were so hard for me. They felt the most unnatural to me. Even though Eric is assisting me on throws, I still use my own rhythm. But the twist requires both of us to be perfectly accurate. If one of us is not 100 per cent accurate, it won't work.

"Pairs usually do the twist first in their programs. The triple twist uses the most explosive power. It's really about having natural unison and timing. If we anticipate the other and it misfires, then all that power you put into it deflates. It's about being relaxed but then having explosive power at the right time. Then making sure Eric catches me and puts me down."

They needed to have the throw triple twist if they wanted to challenge for ISU and Olympic medals. And, it went without saying that they wanted to compete at the Olympics. It wasn't until a journalist asked at Skate Canada in 2010 that they publicly acknowledged they were training for the Olympics. That first season they also wanted to qualify for Worlds and in order to do that, they had to be top two at Canadians.

It seemed like a heady renewal of Eric and Meagan's skating. Every experience through those early years together was a first. Their first time making the world team. Their first time being in the second-last flight or group of skaters at Worlds and being among all the other teams that they had watched on TV. Then the following season they were contenders at competitions. The excitement and momentum just kept building. It was beyond Eric's wildest dreams, as he recalls.

"We did a lot of interesting things," Eric remembers. "In 2012 we finished our short program off with a throw triple flip jump. There was no need for it but we could do it because we were so good at those things. We were just finding ourselves in those years. We had to make everything more consistent than the year before if we wanted to gain ground.

"And as we gained ground, we were skating under just a little bit more pressure. At the Grand Prix events we were in position to win medals for the first time. Going into Canadians knowing that the title would be ours if we skated well—these are different expectations to deal with. It was so exciting.

"We were both so open and willing to learn whatever we could. We were also good at working together to figure stuff out on our own. We couldn't be in a lesson all the time with a coach. We were very much on the same page where if we were working on a new element, we were good at communicating and working on it together."

For the most part Meagan and Eric never fought. They never screamed at the other, or lost control or their tempers on the ice. There were bad days when both were upset, but Eric recalls they never had one of the big fights they had seen other teams experience.

"I think we're both fairly adaptable people and we had a baseline understanding that when we come into the rink, we're there to do our best. There was never a day where I felt that Meagan didn't do her best and I think she feels the same for me. There's no point in getting angry when something isn't working when you know that we're both doing the best we can in that moment.

"Meagan being an extrovert and me being an introvert provided a nice balance. I'm a very easy-going person. I don't get upset easily. I don't like confrontation and I don't like being upset.

"I think that Meagan is definitely more defined in what she likes, wants and needs. If Meagan said she needed to do three triple Lutzes, I was always like, okay. Or if she felt like she wanted to do another long program at the end of the week, I always said yes."

Meagan's high octane drive seemed to push and inspire Eric to do more than he would have, naturally. He describes himself as the type of skater who would consider an element accomplished once he'd executed it once or twice, and wouldn't repeat it over and over. But he also knew it took more than that to get the deep level of training necessary for an athlete to skate clean programs under high pressure. He says they created a balance for one another and throughout their entire career, that remained one of their main strengths.

"We communicate fairly well. When we listen to music, we listen with Julie. Meagan may say, 'I don't feel anything when I listen to this,' and it will be the most beautiful music I've ever heard. We'll be on different pages but again our desire to have what's going to be the best for all of us will always trump everything, and that's the most important thing.

"Even if Meagan didn't feel as strongly about the music I composed for the 2014 Olympics right away, for example, she knew it could be a great program.

"The first time we listened to the Muse music, Meagan really wanted to skate to it and I couldn't see myself skating to rock and roll. But I said, 'Okay, I'm going to do my best and make it work.' And it ended up being great."

They had many conversations about specific changes they were going to make. They discussed their skating and what their goals should be throughout a season. They often came home and reset programs. They had to decide on music, costumes, the huge issue of scheduling and, remarkably, when to take their vacations and for how long.

"There was a lot of communication, but I feel another sort of blessing in disguise was that Meagan and I started to hit our stride and have success a lot later in our careers than other pair teams, on average. A lot of other pair teams start when they are very young. We were doing everything later in our lives when we were adults. What came along with that was a different perspective and a deeper appreciation for what was happening."

Meagan says once they started training together, they were humming along. They had a unique side-by-side jump in the triple Lutz and their singles skating skills. They had two strong programs and thought they could just show up on the Grand Prix circuit and win right away. Meagan says they created an amazing, grand projection for what they thought they could achieve.

Once they began to compete, however, things didn't turn out quite the way that they had first envisioned. The side-by-side triple Lutz jump was working in practice but that didn't automatically translate into a successful jump in competition. Meagan hadn't actually tried that jump for years. Their first Grand Prix was Skate Canada and was a sign of their growing pains. They finished fifth and Meagan recalls they skated terribly. Yet something else emerged from that first year, which was indicative of the direction they would take.

"We always found something to be excited about. You know, Eric had never scored above 100 points before. And we knew that if we worked hard and performed the way we thought we could, we would make it to Worlds that year."

So even though there were bumps along the road the first year, they would come home, address the issues and make it be better the next time. They were always focusing on the next step.

As Meagan and Eric's partnership evolved, Meagan was developing another pairing—she had begun dating Bruno. Meagan says that there isn't much of a story to tell in terms of how it all developed. But one night over Skype, Meagan recounts how their off-ice relationship came about.

Eric and Meagan lived close to each other, and neither was in a serious relationship so they had a lot of free time. They spent time off-ice together and told each other everything. Except, Meagan never told anybody she was dating Bruno.

"I didn't even tell Eric at first. And, we didn't want to tell Richard, that was the main thing. Bruno and I didn't want Richard to know because Bruno was worried Richard would fire him and tell him he couldn't coach at the rink anymore. I was twenty-five years old and Bruno was thirty-five. Age and coaching were not issues for me, but we didn't really know how serious our relationship was so we laid low on it.

"We had started spending time together at Four Continents in 2010, when I knew Craig would be retiring and I was considering other skating partners. Bruno always insisted it would be Eric and I thought that was so weird. Why are you so sure about this? Why are you so eager about this? I feel like that's how we started talking and hanging out more and one thing leads to another."

A week before Canadians in 2011, she finally told Eric. He was so insulted that Meagan hadn't told him sooner, saying, "I can't believe you kept that from me." Shortly after, Bruno and Meagan told Richard.

As it turned out, Richard was fine with the arrangement. Meagan recalls how he told them they were both adults. "You know what you're getting into." But Richard warned them not to bring any drama to his rink.

"Richard was always professional about attitudes. He didn't want any negative energy on his rink. You had to be getting along. If you were fighting with your partner, you didn't come to skate. He doesn't deal with this.

"Eric and Bruno and I all grew together. I feel like we've all been in a relationship together over all these years.

"I never considered leaving Bruno as my coach. Even if things had gotten so bad and we weren't together anymore and we got divorced, he would be the one I'd want to be my coach. He is very knowledgeable. He understands exactly what Eric needs and he understands exactly what I need. He knows us both so well. He knows our skating better than we know our skating. I wouldn't question it. No matter what would happen in our personal life, he is the coach I'd want at the rink and at the boards in competition.

"He was my coach first. We were together for a year and nobody knew it at the rink. Even Eric didn't pick up on this and he knew me as well as anybody. We were always, and we still are, extremely professional at the rink. If anything, we get less attention than his other students. He's made sure to be very fair and respectful to everybody."

But how does it work? The way Meagan describes it, their lives are normal. She and Bruno wake early and walk the dogs. She makes lunches for her husband and herself. For a moment it sounds like there is a division between Bruno, her husband getting the lunch, and Bruno, her coach, who will eat it.

As she says, they go to work and it's work. They come home and some days work comes home with them and some days it doesn't. They've never had a rule about not talking about skating once they left the rink. Skating is such a big part of their lives, it feels to Meagan like they are always talking about it.

Meagan stopped skating in Saint-Leonard in June of 2017. Bruno was working there in the mornings and Meagan still enjoyed hearing how everybody was doing at Saint-Leonard. She enjoyed it when Bruno showed videos of what Kirsten Moore-Towers and Michael Marinaro and the other teams were doing. She missed seeing the progress of other teams and especially of Kirsten and Michael, who were her Olympic teammates. She could still have that connection through Bruno.

"Bruno used to skate competitively when Eric was fifteen. Eric used to think Bruno was so old. He'd say, 'Bruno is twenty-five and he's still skating. That's so old,'" she laughs. "It's funny to look back on that when we are thirty-two and still skating!"

In 2011, at the ripe old ages of twenty-five and twenty-six respectively, Meagan and Eric finished second at Canadians. After the podium ceremony, Meagan skated around the rink wearing her silver medal, telling her parents that it felt like a gold medal. It was the ultimate moment. She doesn't know whether her joy came from winning the actual medal or from the performance.

What Meagan did know that day was that she hadn't skated like that in so long, if ever.

"We were fourth after the short program. Only two pairs teams were going to World Championships. We'd had a terrible practice that morning. I couldn't land anything. I was a mess and was still stuck thinking about the messy short program the night before. While I was waiting for the bus to go back to the hotel, I was by myself backstage. I was crying, but every person who walked by stopped to talk to me. Tracy Wilson talked to me. I left the rink feeling uplifted, supported and encouraged.

"That night we were so nervous when we went into the long program. But we were also so trained and so ready. We kept repeating, 'Just like home. Just like home. We're just back at home.' Our coaches at the boards told us, 'You're at home.' We really tried to put ourselves into the rink back at home where we had done so many great performances."

That was the first time Eric and Meagan ever had to skate as a team under extreme pressure. They had done it before, plenty of times, as individuals and with other partners. But it was the first time for them in a be-all or end-all. Their first season together was going to continue or end in that moment. And they skated an amazing, clean long program. After that, Meagan says their eyes were opened to the fact that they could be great competitors and seize the moment in a clutch situation.

"That skate at Canadians made us confident that we could handle any other difficult pressure-filled situation we might encounter. We felt confident in that moment, even if it was terrifying.

"We had qualified for the world team. It's a dream come true to represent your country and skate at the World Championships. It all came down to the performance. We got that opportunity because we delivered a magical performance in the moment when it mattered the most."

Then it was on to Russia for the World Championships. The tsunami forced the ISU to change location from Japan to Russia. Eric and Meagan were aiming for a top ten finish.

Meagan says the triple twist was still new to them. In the process of learning a double or triple twist, the male skater's nose gets hit; about 90 per cent end up with a broken nose. But this usually happens behind closed doors, back at home at the rink, not for the world to see.

"That night in our short program the twist simply didn't go high enough. I was finishing my rotation when Eric went to catch me. Usually the rotation would be finished with my arms up. Eric would catch me and put me down. But I was finishing the rotation and unravelling when he was getting ready to make the catch.

"We've had that happen at home—and it has happened since then. But usually when we're at home, Eric would be like, 'Oh, my God, oh, my God,' and he'd fall over and be dramatic about it. In that moment at Worlds, I was thinking, 'Oh, my God! Please stay calm.' I didn't know how he'd react."

Eric did stay calm, even as the blood started to stream down his face. They came around the corner of the ice into the signature side-by-side triple Lutz and then missed the jump. They didn't fall, and moved on to the lift. As they went into the lift, Meagan got a good look at Eric. In the moment, Eric didn't know how bad it was. "As we came around the corner of the rink into the jump, my eyes were tearing up from the pain. I was thinking, 'Oh, this isn't fair. I have to do this jump. I can't see, and I couldn't stop.' There is a referee who can stop the program if they feel there's something dangerous happening. We left that in their control. We just kept on going.

"At the end of our program we presented to the judges; every time I turned my head quickly, blood flew. I could see the judges looking at my face. It was a really strange experience. After it all happened, everyone kept asking, 'How did you do that? How did you keep on going?'

"The answer is, you have to. Your adrenaline is so high. And your muscle memory has kicked in. Meagan told me going into that lift that we should stop. I picked up the lift, and the next thing we knew we were at the end of the program. We don't know what happened in between. It was like this strange autopilot mode."

There was a day off between the short and long programs. They were concerned about doing the triple twist again. Meagan says they wondered if they should just do the double. They went with the old adage, and got back up in the saddle. They finished seventh overall, the top Canadian pair.

On the way to dinner that night, a funny thing happened to Eric, who had instantly gained notoriety. Images of the bloody moment can still be found on the Internet.

Meagan Duhamel and Eric Radford with Laura E. Young

"Of course, the accident was all over the news. At dinner, an important-looking Russian man in a suit approached me. He said, 'You are the Canadian that broke his nose, right? I just wanted to let you know that our president had great words to say about your strength today.' Putin was there watching the show that night. I was like, 'No way. Vladimir Putin knows who I am.'"

In the 2011–2012 season, Meagan and Eric skated to Joaquin Romero's "Concierto de Aranjuex" for their short program, and created the Coldplay long program, featuring the songs "Viva La Vida" and "Yellow." They won Canadians for the first time in either of their senior careers. That victory at Canadians unveiled the possibility that they could be successful on the world stage.

Meagan would achieve a dream of hers, having seen her sister skate at Canadians, and having seen the maple leaf shaped podium where the medallists are awarded. Back in 1999, she told her father she would stand on top of that podium one day.

Winning their first national title contributed heavily to building the confidence and conviction Meagan and Eric needed to get to the world podium.

In order to improve, Meagan and Eric set out to earn the levels they had often carelessly left on the table by not, for example, holding their positions long enough to get the levels and collect the points that came with those elements. In their second season, they came up with the Coldplay free skate which made a statement in terms of choreography and innovative style, and created a look that was really theirs.

It would take a few seasons to make the side-by-side triple Lutz their signature. They rarely landed it in competition during the first two seasons. The second season together they were doing triple Salchow jumps in their short program. They were skating clean in the short program all season and then at Worlds the triple Lutz was back in. But they fell on it so they didn't actually land the element.

Their coaches told Meagan and Eric that some people were asking why the skaters were bothering to try the triple Lutz when they could just go for a nice, easier, triple toe jump? Bruno and Richard told them it would pay off when it started to work.

Bruno and Richard were so insistent, saying that Meagan and Eric were going to make mistakes at first, but one day they would win because of that triple Lutz. Bruno would say, "When you're doing something new and it's something so hard, it does take time for trial and error."

Although later, their lifts would be spectacular and seem to cover the entire ice surface, they missed lifts a lot in those early years and thus dropped valuable points. In their first competition, the lift didn't go up and they left behind the seven points that came with it.

Meagan says their timing was off and Eric couldn't do the lift. They each understood that the other was always trying their best, and never sought to blame each other for mistakes. If

Meagan missed a jump in the short program, the skaters would talk later about what they needed to do so that didn't happen again. Clear communication always came after mistakes.

"If one of us fell on an element, it was really that we fell. It doesn't matter if one of us lands it. On the scoresheet it says fall for the team. The mistake is always part of the team, it's never individual.

"That's always the way we've approached it and that's part of our magic and our ability to work together. We have seen a lot of teams that can't work through things in that regard."

The short program of the second season was perhaps the most intricate program that they ever had. That might have been lost on people because it seemed to Meagan and Eric that people thought they were all about the big jumps. But for Eric and Meagan, the Coldplay and the Concierto de Aranjuex programs were detailed programs that went beyond jumping. The following season as well, they were working to be innovative and to chase that second or artistic mark.

The Olympic chatter began about one year before the 2014 Games. Sometimes they would catch themselves dreaming of the possibilities and say, "I really hope Canada gets three pairs at the Olympics so that all the good pairs teams in Canada can go." That way it would be unlike Meagan's experience in 2010 where third place had to sit at home.

While Sochi hovered in a near and possible future, skating was more about the moment and the daily process. That first season was about getting on the world team. The next year was winning Canadians and being top five in the world. They focused on the challenge of finding a way to close the gap between themselves and the teams in front. Meagan focused on the fact that other pairs teams were ten points ahead of them, and turning that around so she and Eric could finish ten points ahead of their competition.

"I always find that part of skating the most satisfying. That's why I am always motivated. I love the grind of working towards something, the grind of what else can I do, how can I be better, how can I find more points, where can I find a way to improve?"

In 2012, Meagan and Eric knew going into Canadians that they had an opportunity to win their first Canadian pairs title. There has always been a certain prestige in winning a Canadian figure skating title. Canada has such an incredibly rich, deep history in the sport. The title is a cachet that opens doors to skating shows and secures teaching spots at seminars around the country.

They had skated well in their short program, until they tripped on the choreography going into their lift. They reset and then Eric lifted Meagan. The technical specialists didn't see it that way and didn't award any points on the lift. Instead the technical panel ruled that the trip up on the choreography counted as part of the lift, because the view was the choreography was the initiation to the lift. So while they sat in first after the short, it wasn't by much, because they had lost six points for the miss, Meagan recalls.

"We were really pissed off, because we could have had a buffer going into the free skate. But now, we were in first with less than a point ahead of three other teams. It made the long program more stressful. We kind of had a chip on our shoulder about that lift going into the long program because we, and our coaching team, truly believed it was an incorrect call.

"We were skating last and I was pacing backstage. I kept saying, 'This is your opportunity and you need to go get it.' We said again to our coaches: 'We're back at home.' That rink became our training centre at home."

They launched the program with a solid triple twist. Then the three-jump combination, which at that time was the triple flip, double toe, double toe. An excitement began building in the rink, increasing after each successful element. They landed the three-jump combination, then spun around into the second jump and landed the triple Salchow. That marked the end of the high-risk elements. The audience was so loud that Meagan couldn't hear Eric call the change of position in their side-by-side spin. She tried to stay calm after the spins but it was tough. They were halfway through the program and just knew: this is it. This was their moment.

They fought the throws a bit but knew there was only the throw triple Salchow and the throw triple flip to land. Easy! Meagan felt like she was ahead of herself, starting the celebration by thinking, "Oh we're going to win. We're going to win."

They had been so nervous going into the skate, but as soon as the music finished, Meagan could relax, knowing they had done enough.

"Then the score came: 129 points, which was the highest we'd ever scored up to that point. Eric was staying calm like he does. He said, 'Wait, the screen is going to show we went into first, watch.' For Eric, the most exciting moment was seeing the screen flash the number one beside our name.

"We've been to every skating competition in the world, and the biggest one is the Canadian Figure Skating Championships. There's an excitement from the fans. They're knowledgeable, enthusiastic and encouraging. The who's who of Canadian figure skating is there, either as an alumnus or a coach or a spectator. You're surrounded by all these familiar faces and familiar stories. So for us at that point in 2012, winning Canadians was the pinnacle of the pinnacle of what we thought we could achieve in our skating careers."

The 2012 World Championships was both a positive and negative experience. Meagan recalls they skated an average short program, but a lot of teams made mistakes that night, so despite falling on the Lutz Meagan and Eric were not out of the running heading into the free skate. They skated a solid long program and were happy with their fifth-place finish.

Narumi Takahashi and Mervin Tran skated for Japan and had trained with Meagan and Eric in Montreal. Bruno and Richard also coached them. The Japanese team won the bronze medal but in doing so they beat Meagan and Eric for the first time. Meagan hates to admit it, but she and Eric had never really considered them as intense competitors. It was a good lesson.

"We were backstage wondering what was going on? They can win a world medal?

"All of a sudden we were thinking that we should have won that world medal. Our goal had been to finish in the top five, but then we were feeling disappointed because we missed an opportunity to win the bronze. If we could have landed that triple Lutz in the short that bronze could have been ours. We had finished four points behind them.

"I felt a little bit awkward with Bruno because I was upset that our teammates had beaten us. But Bruno was on the high of his life because he'd just coached two teams coming top five at Worlds."

Eric and Meagan's results made them realize they had to set their levels and expectations higher. Fifth was no longer good enough. The podium? Yes. If their teammates had found their way to the podium, so could Meagan and Eric. That would become the drive through the 2012–2013 season. Get on the podium at the World Championships.

In order to accomplish this, they had to create great programs and land the side-by-side triple Lutz in the short program. Missing it in the short at the 2012 Worlds had removed Meagan and Eric from the final warm-up group. With the same long program, but skating in the final group, they anticipated they likely would have scored a bit higher and earned enough for the bronze.

After Worlds, Meagan and Eric began working on new short and long programs. They debuted "La Bohème" for the short program, while Philippe Rombi's music from the *Angel* soundtrack seemed to weave a story and lift their long program to a bright finish.

Julie created a high energy short program set to La Bohème. For the long program the team created a more lyrical, romantic style program because they had just come from a high energy crowd pleaser. They looked to try something new, a quieter, more introverted energy, which also meant they would have to skate consistently in that long program or the program wouldn't work as well as it should. It was a nice program but it was the spectacular short program to "La Bohème" that really made the world take notice.

Meagan and Eric began working with an acting coach that season, something they would do off and on for about three years, Meagan remembers.

"It was so out of our comfort zone. She was great but she also wanted us to appear loving and romantic in that long program. And we kept telling her we can't do that. We look ridiculous when we try to do that.

"The Angel program was slow and lyrical. It was a romantic storyline that we were trying to portray. It was nice but it wasn't us. We never went back to that romantic style again. We really excelled in the La Bohème short program. We loved it every single time we skated. The crowd would get into it, and I would be more into it. It was awesome."

Meagan Duhamel and Eric Radford with Laura E. Young

Meagan and Eric found their way to the Grand Prix podium in the first half of the season, taking silver at Skate Canada and at Trophée Eric Bompard in France. They were fourth in the Grand Prix Final. Then it was off to see how they would fare at Canadians.

The night of the pairs long program at the 2013 Canadians, the country's strong tradition in pairs was on full display.

Kirsten Moore-Towers and Dylan Moscovitch skated second last and scored nine points more than Eric and Meagan had ever tallied. Fans were going wild. To add to that, Dylan is Eric's best friend. The competition between the two pairs teams was fierce. Meagan and Eric say they love that they went through their first four years with and against Kirsten and Dylan.

That skate at Canadians saw Meagan and Eric so nervous all day. At lunch the normally positive Meagan sat in despair, feeling like she couldn't do it, couldn't do anything. The two teams were tied, essentially, as the point difference was so small.

Backstage Meagan and Eric kept the focus on themselves, reminding each other that they were back at home. Meagan could feel the crowd's energy.

"Right before Kirsten and Dylan's program was over, we went through the curtain to get to the boards so we could step on the ice when they finished. When we walked through the curtain their coach looked me in the eye and said 'Yes!' as he fist-pumped and screamed.

"At that moment I just said, 'Fuck it.' I closed my eyes and imagined that the crowd was cheering for us and encouraging us. Except they weren't. They were giving Dylan and Kirsten a standing ovation because they'd just had an amazing skate." Then they stepped on the ice to perform one of the hardest long programs they'd ever had to skate. They opened the program with a miss on the triple twist. Meagan completed 2.5 rotations and stopped rotating. The catch was awkward. They looked at each other and said, "That's okay." It didn't unravel them and they moved on to the triple Lutz. After that it felt like clockwork.

When they got off the ice, Meagan asked Bruno if they had done enough to win. Bruno always knew exactly how they would score; even when they didn't want him to know because it was bad. But it was so close between the top two Canadian teams. He looked at them and said, "I don't know. I don't know what the judges are going to do." So, they waited, Meagan recalls.

"It was a complete surprise when we got our marks and went into first place. When we go back and watch those two programs back to back, it was an amazing moment for Canadian pairs skating. We have so much respect for the fight Kirsten and Dylan put up. But it made us so much better because they were doing that. Those were the most amazing days, when we were battling them. We knew that they were having a great season. They had great programs. They wanted it. They didn't like not winning the year before."

Eric says they had never used the word "defend," and had only ever said they wanted to win the national title. "There's nothing to defend. It's all starting fresh every time. That mentality really has helped us many times in our career. Each national title has its own story, feeling, value, and worth. The first time is always the best, but that second one is definitely amazing in its own right. In a way it was a lot more difficult than the first time.

"It was like a movie. It was the ultimate pressure and we had to go and do it in that moment, when it counted the most, and we did it. Those moments define a career and lead to all the opportunities we've had."

It's a tried and true sports cliché that it's a lot harder to defend a title than to win it. Once an athlete has had a taste of being a Canadian champion, then the athlete knows the possibility is there and wants to taste it again. For Eric, knowing what he's capable of and the fear that he won't maximize that opportunity in that moment adds to the nerves and pressure.

There were two really strong teams in Canada that season. Eric and Meagan think had they not been up against another team that had scored nine points higher than they ever had, they probably wouldn't have felt as much pressure as they did.

The motivation from day one of the 2012-2013 season was to be on the world podium in their home country as the 2013 Worlds were being held in London, Ontario. The other motivation was the fact that if their teammates, Narumi and Mervin, could do it, then so could they.

Two weeks after winning their second Canadian title, Eric and Meagan won their first Four Continents title, setting new personal best scores in the long and short programs. But Meagan remembers they didn't appreciate it as much as they might have because they lost the long program to Dylan and Kirsten by one point.

Then they came home to better prepare for the 2013 Worlds. Meagan remembers they prepared by simulating different scenarios to replicate the draw for the order in which the teams would compete.

"You hate skating first in the long because you rush your six-minute warm-up. You're tired and then you have to perform your program. So we simulated skating first in the long program a couple of times as we went into the World Championships; lo and behold we skated first in the long program at Worlds.

"In the short program, everyone was skating well: the Russians, the Germans. Then Eric and I had a great skate. It was electric. We scored our personal best for the short. Then we saw a number two come up. We never even imagined being number two at Worlds. We thought the Russians would be first or second with the Germans and that third spot would be available.

"But all of a sudden we had beaten the Germans in the short and they had skated cleanly. That was another excitement. This was, 'Oh my God, what's going on?' That was crazy. We were on a huge high," Meagan says.

Then they had to settle down and prepare to skate the long program the next day. They again lost some levels on the lifts and for some other minor issues. One of Eric's double toe jumps was downgraded. They were slightly off on the throw Lutz at the end of the program but they completed the elements. Their job was done. Now they just had to sit and wait and watch.

Eric opted to retreat to the men's change room. Bruno left. Meagan stood by herself watching the Russians skate, thinking, "If the Russians beat me, I want to see what they do."

The Russian team made one mistake but they were still skating well until they completely missed a lift that was worth seven points. That was it! Meagan knew that she and Eric had done it, that they were third before the Russians had even finished.

She went running to find Eric and Bruno, so at the moment when it was announced they were third, the television cameras wouldn't catch her standing there alone.

"Eric wanted to know if I was sure. I said, 'They completely missed a lift, there's no way they can pass us.' Eric still wanted to be sure.

"Then we were able to appreciate that we had really done it. There was some disbelief that we had actually climbed up the ladder like we had the last three years.

"I remember at Worlds in London that year, thinking that every goal we set, we reached it. We wanted to make Worlds; we wanted to be top five; we wanted to be on the podium. We were just manifesting everything we've ever dreamt of in skating."

Eric and Meagan also took a moment to revel in being lucky enough to be on the podium at home in Canada, too. It would ultimately be the only World Championships that they ever competed in at home. Meagan says it was such a magnificent one. They stood on the podium with the gold medallists Tatiana Volosozhar and Maxim Trankov of Russia, and the silver medallists Aljona Savchenko and Robin Szolkowy, from Germany—their idols and competitors.

Two weeks later, Meagan and Eric competed at the ISU World Team Trophy. Then they joined the Stars on Ice Tour for the first time. There wasn't a point where they could stop and really appreciate that they were world bronze medallists and two-time Canadian champions invited to tour. Their schedule moved quickly. Soon it was time to choreograph their Olympic programs.

Meagan and Eric recall how no one talked much about them in the beginning. They weren't a threat, they were a little off the radar, Meagan reflects. "But as soon as we started being successful, of course then the critics come, which is sadly the way it is in life. At the World Team Trophy a Russian coach started talking about us in interviews, saying how terrible we are, how we didn't match and how we couldn't skate. This coach wanted to know what coach would think about pairing two skaters like this, like us, together."

"I am pretty thick-skinned and can take things with a grain of salt. I wouldn't say I have a lot of confidence in myself, but I wasn't sensitive enough that people's comments wore me down."

They well knew that they were working as hard as possible and doing everything they could. They heeded the advice and the feedback from judges and officials, which, as Meagan and Eric say, was the most important feedback.

And, as they continued to seek a signature look, they were in a phase of trial and error. During that phase they tried a heavily theatrical long program, skating to music by Danny Elfman from the soundtrack to the 2010 movie *Alice in Wonderland*. Since people said they didn't match, they deliberately tried to be different. Finding themselves took time but the La Bohème short program, the Coldplay long program and eventually the Muse long programs were solid signs that they could create a unique and winning look. For Meagan it was about evolution.

"You don't want to stick with that style all the time. We were trying to be innovative and sometimes when you take that route you aren't always successful.

"Our style basically became something that showed us being authentically Meagan and authentically Eric. Neither of us had to change. We just had to find a way to meet on a middle ground. How can we make Meagan the best she can be, and make Eric the best he can be? How can we meet in the middle, as opposed to one of us trying to go too far to the one end? That's what we came to for our style; we don't know if there's a word for that style. It's us, it's organic. It's raw and it's us."

They first touched that raw and organic, original "us" in the 2013–2014 season. Their music for their Olympic short program grew from being just "Paul's Song," a tribute to Eric's late coach Paul Wirtz, to "Tribute," a composition that reflected their appreciation of everyone who had supported their careers, from their families to their fans.

Eric originally composed the piece for piano and recorded his own version into a computer program, complete with an orchestral arrangement. Considering that Eric created it during the numb, unreal days after Paul Wirtz's death in April 2006, the melody is at its core hopeful, sounding as if it looks forward and up.

Once Eric had dreamed of composing music that he would skate to at an Olympic Games, combining his two main passions. But who would have thought things like this were even possible? Then as he looked up music conductors in Montreal on the Internet, his dream was about to come true.

"I wanted the music for Sochi to have a strong emotional tie. It needed to mean something, not just be some random piece of music for what, at the time, we thought would be our one and only Olympics."

Eric knew the melodic theme would transfer well to orchestra. He floated the idea over to Julie who was totally open to it. Eric didn't want to approach Meagan until he had something more concrete, a plan.

His random online search led him to Louis Babin. Eric called Louis and told him how he had a song that he would like orchestrated for the Olympics. Louis said, "Of course; let's see what you can do." Eric says they decided to turn it into an orchestral version.

"It was a process. It was like trying to fit a bunch of pieces into a puzzle at the same time. It was a group effort between the three of us. Julie was involved with the highlights and lowlights with the music as well as where we would insert the skating elements with the music. I was involved in the type of feeling and the instrumentation and the harmonies I wanted. Louis took the beats per minute and structured the music to make sure everything fit Julie's and my ideas.

"There were times when Louis would write it out for synthesized sounds. I brought that one version in and played it for Meagan. I think Meagan and Julie had a hard time getting past those synthesized sounds because I could see it in their faces: 'Oh, my God. What is this?' But they were still very supportive."

Eric told the team he didn't want them to fear telling him if they weren't feeling the music like he was. His first goal, before writing a piece to skate to, was to have the best program at the Olympics.

But the magical moment came when they went into the studio and the orchestra was there. They ran through the first ten to twelve bars of music, only about twenty seconds. Hearing it come to life was life-changing for Eric.

"In that moment I knew that I wanted to write and record music like this. It was magical. Electricity was going through my body. I had chills. Julie and I looked at each other and we knew it was going to work."

Even if Eric and Meagan had never skated to "Tribute", Eric would've remained proud of the music. He agrees it took some measure of courage to put it out there, given how crass and nasty people can be when it comes to judging. As Meagan and Eric gained traction and landed on the podium, the critics were coming for them. Not only would Eric be skating, the skating world would be listening to his music, which in a way he felt was an even deeper part of his soul than his skating. He told himself, 'Okay, Eric, just prepare yourself. Not everyone is going to love it.'

"I remember the first time we did our run-through at Skate Canada to 'Tribute.' Even though it was a practice session, there were a lot of people in the audience. When we started I was totally aware that everybody was hearing my song. I could feel a little bit of insecurity coming through. What are people thinking? I've only had positive comments."

"Tribute" was recorded in one session in April 2013. It was no small project. It took a large chunk of financing, which Eric paid for himself, and scheduling to take it to a level where he felt it was presentable enough to be at the Olympics. The short program for the Olympics was choreographed before they went on vacation at the end of May 2013.

2014 SOCHI OLYMPICS: AN OLYMPIC REALITY CHECK WITH A SILVER LINING

The resort city of Sochi lies about 1,600 kilometres south of Moscow, nestled on the eastern shores of the Black Sea at the base of the Caucasus Mountains. In February of 2014, it was the site of the most expensive Winter Olympics to date—a cost of over $51 billion. One Olympic cycle later, in 2018, the cost to Russia would also include medals and overall placement lost in the final medal count, not to mention the fall of the once mighty Russian sports empire. It was as if the 2014 Olympics was the pinnacle of Russian athletic prowess. They would win the games' medal count at thirty-three, well ahead of the American, Norwegian and Canadian teams.

By 2016 the McLaren Report was the latest in damning the Russian athletic program, alleging that the Russian government had sanctioned systemic doping in its athletes at the Sochi Games. The Russians lost thirteen medals with nine later reinstated. Perhaps the worst of it for the Russians was they had to compete as OAR, the Olympic Athletes of Russia, at the 2018 Games and dress neutrally with no indication of their nation's colours or flag.

Prior to the 2014 Games, the media reported a rash of problems, from packs of roaming stray dogs to corruption to the anti-gay law, which led many world leaders to boycott the games. Early arrivals at the actual games had to contend with brown water from the taps, no warm water, and holes in the walls in some of the hotels and athlete accommodations at the Black Sea resort.

But still, it was the Olympics! The secret dream every athlete harbours at one point, and, as with most Olympics, things settled down after a few days and the focus was finally on the athletes and the competition.

Four years earlier Meagan had joined the rest of Canada in an Olympic coma, watching the Vancouver Games from her couch; Eric had joined his brother Richard in Australia. Both thought their competitive careers were done. In 2014, they were marching behind the Canadian flag at the opening ceremony in Sochi and standing on the podium wearing an Olympic medal, another moment so many athletes can only ever imagine.

Eric says, as world bronze medallists, they knew it was possible they could end up on the podium, perhaps even in their individual event.

"Still, there were many strong teams: Pang Qing and Tong Jian of China had won world bronze in 2011. The Germans were there, and Russia had three strong pairs teams. We had beaten Pang and Tong at Worlds in 2013 but you could never count them out because they could step it up at any moment. If we were going to end up on the podium, it would be quite a feat. We were going to have to skate very, very well."

Even though the word "Olympics" seemed to permeate everything that year, Eric and Meagan weren't preoccupied with thinking that they were off to the Olympics and that they had to win a medal. But, they felt like they might have put some unnecessary pressure on themselves as they prepared for Sochi.

Eric took extra precautions to avoid any injuries or illness. When he crossed the street he would look both ways twice. When he walked down and up stairs, he would hold onto the railing so he didn't trip. He wore gloves when he rode the Metro in Montreal so he wouldn't get sick.

"We'd be at the gym on the rowing machine and every row was 'Olympics, Olympics,' giving it our all, at all times, because we really wanted to go to the Olympics knowing that we had literally done everything possible, so that even if we had a bad skate, we would know that we had given it everything we had. It was a different level of training and preparation that season."

Meagan says much was unknown about Sochi in terms of their schedule. "We had never gone to the Olympics. We didn't know if we were doing the short or the long in the team event, or were we doing the entire thing? We didn't find out until two weeks before the Olympics. That season we had a long program and we hadn't been competing well because we weren't comfortable with the material. There were so many things going on."

Heading into Sochi, Meagan and Eric were world medallists and had been Canada's number one team internationally for a few years. They knew they were going to go to the Olympics so they weren't feeling the stress of having to qualify or knowing that they wouldn't qualify at all.

The question became whether they would come first or second. Who would be the third team that qualified with Meagan and Eric, and Kirsten and Dylan? (It would ultimately be Paige Lawrence and Rudi Swiegers of Saskatchewan).

Knowing they were going well ahead of time relieved some of the pressure. All season long, if something came up about the Olympics, they could speak as though they knew they were going instead of well, maybe. Their parents could start organizing their trip instead of having to wait until two weeks before. Nationals are usually held about three weeks before the Olympics. It's a quick turnaround if you don't know you're going, as Meagan says.

"I don't really know if there was a big ah-ha moment until I was in Sochi, when I knew I was actually going to the Olympics. Now that I think about it, I feel sad that I didn't have this moment where there was a big breakthrough: we did it. We qualified. It's a little bittersweet, because we knew all along that we would be going."

That season, Meagan injured her right shoulder falling on a throw early in September. Initially, it was thought that she had separated it, but it was a partial separation that caused a lot of pain. She needed her right arm for the death spiral that was a required element in the short program. They couldn't just choose a different death spiral that might not be as hard on her shoulder. Instead the injury was continuously aggravated throughout the season. Her time away from training was spent dealing with the injury. As she never had a MRI, she could not be sure if anything was torn in her shoulder. There were nights where she couldn't lift her arm unless she lifted it with her left hand.

Every day Meagan and Eric would do that death spiral and Meagan would grit her teeth. Tears would be forming in her eyes. She could not wait for the season to be done so she never had to do that particular death spiral again.

The shoulder also hurt on the lasso lift and there were times when her shoulder seemed to grind and vibrate through her arm, then her hand and into Eric's hand. Meagan recalls that she spent most of the Olympic season trying to keep her shoulder hanging on as long as possible.

"When I look back, that year, leading into the Sochi Olympics, I remember we were also getting drug-tested like crazy. At least twice a month, the random doping agents were at our doors at six o'clock in the morning. We hadn't experienced that before. They usually sought out more high-level or high-profile athletes. Eventually we knew the drug testers' voices from outside the door. Oh yeah, it's you. Again.

"We skated really well at Nationals that year, again in a close battle with Kirsten and Dylan. That was a nice moment, feeling that we'd had this great skate. Then everything started. We had all these team meetings. At one point, Skate Canada left all us athletes together to speak among ourselves. Scott Moir took over the conversation. Scott is always really excited, really optimistic and pumped up. He was talking to us and getting everybody going. He was a veteran, having been to the Olympics before, with Tessa Virtue and Patrick Chan. There was a lot of excitement about competing in that team event, because we knew we had a serious chance to win a medal in that competition."

The skaters arrived in Sochi at 10 o'clock at night and received Team Canada clothing. When Meagan returned to her room at midnight, doping control was waiting in her room. She was taken to a random building in the Olympic Village. Usually if she could not provide a proper sample—if her urine was too diluted, for example—the officials would follow and stay with her until she did. If she was at home, they would go to the rink with her.

In Sochi, Meagan had to stay in the building until she had provided a sample. At three in the morning Meagan was still sitting on a bench drinking apple juice. She asked the testers to come back to her room and wait while she slept. Then she'd provide her morning sample. They said no. This seemed odd to Meagan, who was used to being followed until she could provide a sample. In Sochi, this wasn't even the Olympic committee's doping control, which also seemed strange. The more she thought about it, the sketchier it seemed.

It seemed like the Sochi Olympics were like that. Some experiences were bizarre, others pleasantly surprising. When the team arrived in Russia, the volunteers were helpful and smiling, accommodating and nice. As Eric recalls, that's not what he remembered from his limited experience in Russia.

"We had been in the Metro of Moscow where no one was smiling and the energy was cold and stoic. In Sochi the warmth was different than what we had been anticipating. The security was super smooth and comfortable. Everything for the athletes, despite what people were hearing in the media, was great.

"It really was something to be at our first Olympics after dreaming about it for so long. You do end up walking around realizing that you're at the Olympics. It's really happening right this second. The energy was incredible. It wasn't like a regular figure skating competition. You see the Olympic rings everywhere. There were so many athletes all wearing their team gear. You feel part of the Team Canada club and you become part of something really big. You'd be in the food hall with all the other athletes talking to other people, not just the skaters. The living quarters were not like being in a hotel room where you live out of your suitcase. You turn these quarters into your home for the next two or three weeks."

The morning Eric and Meagan arrived, they were riding the bikes Canadian Tire had provided for the Canadian athletes. After lunch, they were biking back to the Village, just looking around, soaking up the electricity in the air. Eric recalls how it felt the same as it did when they stood on the podium, only it was a constant current and charge of electricity. The partners looked at each other and said, "Can you believe we're at the Olympics?"

In that moment, Eric remembers Meagan saying that she already wanted to do another Olympics. Eric already knew that he was all in for another one. They hadn't even started competing and they both wanted to do it all over again. Eric says they were both serious about staying on for another four-year cycle.

It was also a novel experience for the skaters to find themselves several ranks down on the athlete-as-celebrity hierarchy. At a regular skating competition, there is only figure skating and the fans approach the skaters, who are the stars. Not so at the Olympics, as Eric recalls, where the National Hockey League players were the alpha athletes, in what would become their last Olympics for the foreseeable future. "When you go to the Olympics, we become the fans and the NHL players become the famous ones.

"I didn't really follow hockey that much. I knew who Sidney Crosby was, so I did recognize him, although Sidney Crosby in sweat pants in the Olympic Village looks different than Crosby from a NHL game on TV. It was really funny to see how all the other guys on the skating team were man-crushing on the hockey players. I couldn't imagine what it was like for the hockey players to have people asking them for photos all the time."

When the time came to go to the rink, it was back to work. Obviously everyone knows that ice is ice and it hurts to land on it. But for Eric, like most people who are on ice skates more than actual shoes, there are nuances and the ice feels different at different competitions. Eric prefers soft ice, which some skaters don't like because it can feel almost sticky and it doesn't run well. But Eric has better control on soft ice.

The ice in Sochi felt crispy and hard and Eric would always feel like he was skating on top of it, not into the ice, especially in the practice rink. When he pressed for a really deep edge, he felt like his blade was going to slip. In the actual competition rink, it was a little softer and felt comfortable.

Going into the team event on February 6, Meagan and Eric only had to skate the short program. They had been practising well, and their phase of the team event played out perfectly. As they sat backstage they felt incredibly nervous. While there was no pressure from outside forces, they felt the new pressure to perform and do their job for the team. The Canadian team was strong across all four disciplines and was in the mix for the gold medal.

Leading off for Team Canada, Eric and Meagan laid down what Eric calls "a great, great skate." It was an amazing moment. Every time they were on the ice, in practice and competition, they wanted to live this Olympic moment.

But skating at the Sochi Olympics was different from every other skating event they had been to up to that point. The crowd was something else. When Meagan and Eric went on the ice for the warm-up, the Russian teams were announced and the crowd was deafening. No one had heard cheering that loud before—a roar that seemed to shake all the skaters. Eric says they still talk about it.

"Fortunately, we skated second. We could regroup backstage so we retreated into our little bubble where it was just the two of us, all our usual conversations. We talked to each other a lot. When we returned to the ice we were in the right head space where we needed to be.

"It's just one of those moments where it all happens perfectly, the way you've always visualized it. In the footwork sequence, when everything was done and we were nearing the end, we each took a split second to allow ourselves the thought that, 'I'm skating in the Olympics right now. I'm passing over the Olympic rings on the ice right now.' "

Then it was right back into concentration mode. Eric and Meagan finished the footwork sequence and went into the last death spiral that aggravated her shoulder. The Canadian team in the kiss and cry area was yelling so loudly that it made Eric and Meagan smile as they skated. When they hit the ending position, they had had their Olympic moment in the great, clean short program. They took their bows and headed to the kiss and cry area to await the scores. Everyone was celebrating.

And for good reason. Heading into Sochi, Team Canada was in the running for a medal, possibly even the gold. The strategy then held that Tessa and Scott would be in the top two in ice dancing with their arch rivals Meryl Davis and Charlie White of the United States. Patrick Chan was expected to be in the top two in men's singles, as well.

But as soon as the competition started, Meagan and Eric recall, the Russians were scoring higher than they normally did. It was apparent rather quickly that Canada was no longer in the race for the gold medal. The battle was on for the silver with the Americans who had also iced a strong team across all four disciplines.

Later, the memory of their teammate Kevin Reynolds' long program would become etched forever on Eric's Olympic highlight reel. The Canadian skating team had squeezed their lithe, surprisingly petite bodies into the team box, all friends, travel partners, rivals who had come up through the ranks in Canada for most of their careers. They sat cheering Kevin on as he skated a clean long program with three quadruple jumps. Eric says they were so proud of him.

"We were so thrilled that we could share that with all of our best friends. We had really needed him to beat a lot of the other skaters. And he did.

"For what it's worth, one of the lowest moments I ever felt in skating came next. Evgeni Plushenko skated next for Russia. He performed one quadruple jump, missed a jump and had many errors on his landings throughout his program. Somehow he still beat Kevin's score.

"In that moment I remembered our coach Richard saying that the Olympics aren't a real competition. The Olympics are more political than other competitions because there's so much more money involved. At the time, I thought it was a weird way of looking at the Olympics, but here we were at the Olympics, wondering if any of this was real. There was no way that Plushenko's performance, as good as he was during his career, should have beaten the performance Kevin gave. We saw no logical justification for his score based on our knowledge of figure skating. We were both thinking it was a joke. How does that even happen?

"There ended up being so many of those moments at those Olympics. I left thinking the skating portion of the Olympics wasn't even a real competition. It wasn't about the best skate of the day. It was a fascinating lesson in how high the Russians could score."

At a Winter Olympics, many medal ceremonies are held in a row so the Canadians lined up with the other medallists from other sports in the waiting area. Meagan and Eric trained at the same gym as the short-track speed skaters in Montreal, and were backstage with Charles Hamelin, the short-track speed skater, congratulating one another on their medals.

The Canadian and American skating teams were also celebrating. The Americans had won the bronze and there were many friends between the teams. There was a lot of proverbial pinching themselves and asking, "Can you believe this? We're about to stand on the podium at the Olympics."

Eric remembers standing on the victory podium, the Russian anthem playing, and looking for their families in the front row. "We were smiling at them, mouthing, 'I can't believe this.' It was a really nice moment. They looked so proud, and we were satisfied with that silver medal, especially because we had delivered such a great performance to help the team win silver."

Understandably sleep was hard to find. Usually the relief and comfort after skating the short program are effective sleep aids. Then the skaters prepare for the long program. In Sochi, it was back to the short program in the individual event and they had just won an Olympic medal to boot.

They were caught between preparing to compete again and the body's automatic relaxing after the first competition was over and done. In the end Eric says they just did their best. If they fell asleep at 3 a.m. and had to be up at 7 a.m., then they dealt with it. Maybe they drank an extra coffee that morning. Out on the ice, they were ready, regardless. Anything can happen in the moment, he reflects and all you can do is your best. "That feeling or philosophy underlines everything, regardless of how much preparation you put in."

Meagan says they had never practised or prepared for what would come next, the wave of emotion and exhaustion that coursed through them. "After we received our silver medals we were caught between feeling that we should enjoy the moment and preparing for the so-called 'real' competition, with the pairs up first. We received our medals at night and the next day we had to gear up to compete in our individual event.

"It felt like we were living in a weird time warp with an adrenaline shift. You're on top of the world with an Olympic medal; then, you're switching to the mindset where you know you have to compete at that level again, if not better. We had never practised that scenario. There's no competition where you do a team event then an individual event. It was like jumping in cold water for the first time.

"And, it didn't really help us after the team event had finished that we were left with a bitter taste in our mouths over some of the results we felt may not have been accurate. Then our mindset shifted. Really, who cares what we do? We're not even going to get a medal anyway. Our energy went sour."

In the individual competition, they skated a nice short program, but lost some levels on the throw twist and on the death spiral. The judges decided that the Canadians hadn't caught the triple twist smoothly enough. They also said they didn't hold the death spiral long enough, which angered Meagan and Eric because they reviewed the video of the program and counted the mandatory three rotations. They were scored for a level two on the death spiral; three days earlier, they had received a level four. To this day they can't understand what the difference was between the elements from one program to the next.

That discrepancy in the judging cost one point, set them in fifth, and ultimately knocked the pair out of the final flight and final warm-up group for the Olympic free skate where there was a better shot at a medal.

Their energy was already sour after the team event and it may well have affected how they performed in the individual competition. Eric and Meagan don't blame their final seventh place finish only on that. At the end of the day, they didn't deliver a good long program. But all of these factors may have contributed to the skaters not having the right attitude for the long program, Meagan reflects.

"If we had been competing at home in Canada, the crowd would have been more enthusiastic for us. In Sochi, we were always in a warm-up with Russians. It was like we were stepping on the ice in the middle of a hockey game. The noise and the chanting—it was still unlike anything we'd ever heard at a skating competition. We did the draw for the order we'd be skating. We were hoping we wouldn't skate after a Russian pair. Of course, what did we get? We drew to skate after the Russians.

"In the Olympic final free skate, oddly enough we started the program really well. We landed a great triple twist. Our side-by-side triple Lutz was one of the best we've ever done. But when we came to the side-by-side triple Salchow jumps, I missed it. Again. All season in competition, the Salchow had been failing me. It had become a mental thing by this point. In practice, I never missed it. We changed the jump combination and put it earlier in the program. We tried everything we could, but there was such a mental barrier against that jump that season."

So when she fell on the side-by-side Salchow in Sochi, it was really disappointing but hardly a surprise. They still had half the long program to go and knew it was over. The shot at the medal was gone after the short program. But now they were not even going to have that great skate, that Olympic moment they wanted. They stepped out of the throw near the end. The side-by-side spin was a little off. Even the final ending position was a little shaky. The program finish was lacklustre because their energy was weak.

They sought comfort with their families. Already Eric knew they would finish seventh—not terrible but not as good as they could have been. As the cliché goes: could have, should have, would have. After talking to reporters, he changed and made his way back to watch the final skaters. The Olympics were over.

"I texted my boyfriend at the time, Normand. 'I need to see you.' He had gone to Canada House but told me he was running back. Then it was like a scene from a movie. The crowd was going wild because the Russian skaters were in the final group. All this was happening and I was already so removed from it. I found Normand backstage and we went behind a pillar on the concourse. I sat down and started crying. I had done everything I possibly could and this was the way it would be. I had my cry, kind of regrouped and then went back into the stands to see how things were finishing up with the rest of the competition."

What Eric would realize is that the Olympics are not necessarily about placement. It's about how close an athlete comes to doing their best or doing what they know they are capable of doing. For the skaters out on the ice during the long program, it's all about survival and doing one's best. There's not a lot of time to stop and contemplate anything. It all happens in the moment.

So, Eric recalls that when their scores came up, initially they thought they were okay with the result. After all, they had just skated a long program at the Olympics. They accepted this was the skate they had on that day.

When the pair won their world titles, it was exciting to be world champions, but for Meagan and Eric, the real story is being out there and doing their best in the moment. In their Olympic moment in Sochi, they didn't do their best.

Eric had perhaps imagined what it would be like to have a bad skate at the Olympics. But for the most part, like any young athlete growing up in a sport, he spent more time imagining the complete opposite: skating clean, having a standing ovation, then winning a medal at the Olympics. When it didn't happen, there was such disappointment. As Eric learned, that's reality.

"I remember doing an interview a couple of days after our event. I was asked how I would sum up my Olympic experience. I remember saying I had the excitement of everything that happened in the team event and I have an Olympic medal, which so many athletes dream of winning. I'm lucky to have one.

"Then I had the disappointment of coming seventh in the individual pairs event and not having the great skate I wanted to have. They cancelled each other out and left me in the middle feeling numb. A seventh for somebody can be amazing but when you know your potential is third or even top five, and you come seventh, then you missed your potential and that's where the disappointment comes from."

Meagan cried in the arms of her family after her event. Her brother Johnny sought to console her, trying to lighten the moment by saying without her, the Duhamels wouldn't be treated like celebrities; they wouldn't even be in Russia.

She felt she had done everything right, maybe even that she deserved that great Olympic skate.

"But it doesn't matter how much you think you deserve something, you have to take the moment and you have to do it. I was in a state of, 'Poor me, pity me,' a state I'd already been in after the team event when I was frustrated with some of the judging in the other disciplines.

"That was probably the angriest I've ever been in my life, when I watched an amazing skate like Kevin Reynold's program lose to Plushenko's three-error program in the team event. I guess I just lived too much in a poor-me state at the Olympics and that affected my ability to perform well, because I know I'm capable."

Meagan had never envisioned her Olympic experience finishing with Eric and herself atop the podium. She did want to have a great moment, though. She felt like it was right there to grab and she couldn't reach for it. When she left the ice after what she thought would be their final skate at an Olympics, she didn't feel proud of herself. She felt disappointed.

Meagan remained dejected for the rest of their stay in Sochi. That damn triple Salchow. She had been landing it since she was thirteen years old and it had let her down that entire season, and especially at the Olympics. There was a lot of frustration with that.

She wasn't mad about being beaten; Kirsten and Dylan were always chasing Meagan and Eric. They'd had two great skates at the Olympics, were the top Canadian pair, and were over the moon. They had placed fifth. They were enjoying the Olympics. Meagan remembers feeling so jealous that her teammates had lived the Olympic experience that she had wanted, too.

They remained in Sochi for two weeks after the Olympics. During that time Meagan met many people and heard stories from different athletes. One day while she was sitting in the cafeteria, she met an American speed skater who was so happy about his race. She asked him how he'd done and he said, "Oh, it was so great. I came fifteenth!"

"He was so proud that he'd had the best race of his life. In that moment I realized what the Olympics are about. But it reminded me even more that I didn't get to have what the Olympics are all about."

After competing, Eric and Meagan watched other events. Eric lucked into tickets for the women's hockey final, but, with his limited knowledge of hockey, he thought the game was over at 2-0 for the Americans late in the third period. He commented as much to Johnny Duhamel, who was beside him at the game, and Johnny told him there was still plenty of time. Eric thought, "Yeah, right," and looked at his phone, completely missing Canada's first goal in the Canadians' ultimate comeback and gold-medal victory.

They also practised for the upcoming Worlds and made changes to their programs, simplifying elements, adjusting the throw twist and altering the entry to the death spiral. They changed the order of elements to put the triple Salchow earlier in the program, to see if Meagan would be able to land it.

"Once we got home and started training, we figured we could right our wrongs from the Olympics at the upcoming World Championships. We were only focused on going to Worlds and skating better than we had in Sochi," Meagan says.

They had lived the highest highs and lowest lows and for Meagan, anyway, there was lingering disappointment. They took a week off and then started practising slowly, an hour each day.

Eric says other skaters had told them that skating the World Championships after the Olympics is hell. And it was. "For the first time ever in my career I was completely defeated and lacking motivation. During the March break, there was hardly anyone on the ice at the rink in Montreal. We had just completed a run-through of our program and all I wanted to do was leave. I did not want to be at the rink anymore. It was the first time I'd ever felt emptiness while I was skating.

"But as usual we kept our heads down. We've always been really good at learning from each competition. The focus was on looking forward to what was coming.

"When that shift starts to happen, all the regrets and what ifs start to fade and become positive what ifs. What if we go out and land on the podium at Worlds again? That shift happened for us and we started to move forward. Having not skated a great long program at the Olympics ultimately fuelled us to train for Worlds."

Meagan added another injury to the long list of injuries she'd sustained over her career- this time to her head. "It started with simple crossovers. We were hand in hand when I fell. Eric was so close that he jumped over top of me, trying to stop himself from completely running into me. But he managed to slice my head with his blade. At first we didn't even think he'd cut me. I got up to keep skating but then our coach and Eric saw all the blood. I needed several stitches to close the wound to my head."

They trained the next day and then jetted to Worlds shortly thereafter. In what Meagan describes as an interesting little hiccup, she was skating with stitches in her head at Worlds, because the doctor couldn't get them out. The doctor managed to pull one out but they had to wait to see if the others would come out on their own.

They found redemption at Worlds in Japan that year, and skated one of their career-best short programs; in the long program, they fell—yet again—on the triple Salchow. This time though, Meagan stood up like it was nothing and continued to perform as if the fall had never happened. They claimed the bronze again.

Meagan says when they were on the podium they reminded each other to enjoy the amazing moment. Once again they were on the world podium, and again it had been a close battle with Dylan and Kirsten, who came fourth.

"We have to admit that we were happy to beat them after they had just beaten us at the Olympics. That was a little bit of redemption, as well. That's the competitor in us. We had no idea that they were going to retire after that."

Meagan and Eric came home and toured with Stars on Ice. The plan was to skate for another year. They also learned that back home, the fact of having any Olympic medal overpowers the actual colour of the medal for their fans. "It's an Olympic medal. We would visit schools with other Olympians and the people we'd meet were happy to see the medal. They all wanted to see and hold it. That was amazing," Eric says.

"Perhaps the only people who cared about the colour were ourselves. And again, coming back to how what you did in that moment resulted in what you got. If you got a gold medal, it's because you really did your best in the moment."

Instead of a week or two, Meagan and Eric took off the entire month of June. Meagan went home to Lively, then on to Chicago. She had bought a condominium in Boucherville, Quebec, after the Olympics and was still unpacking and setting up home with Bruno. Meagan moved in right after Worlds finished. It was a busy time. She was getting ready to focus on other aspects in her life. She did not want to live her life on another four-year cycle.

It's fun to think that Meagan and Eric met in a café somewhere in Vieux Montreal and discussed their future over coffee and soy lattes. Meagan will laugh at the café image years later because there were no big meetings. There was no official discussion; instead, they decided to go for it and finally add the throw quadruple Salchow to their repertoire. She says that element became their motivation to continue.

Meagan Duhamel and Eric Radford with Laura E. Young

"We would take everything one competition at a time, so we could appreciate each competition as it was. It's just the 2015 Worlds. It's 2016 Skate Canada. We never talked further than each year. We were more specific. It was, 'Let's do a throw quad,' which meant, 'Let's do another season.' I didn't even discuss continuing for another Olympics with Bruno.

"We kept rolling along. We returned from a long vacation rejuvenated and refocused on ourselves. We both seemed to reset over our vacation, but separately, without talking to each other. We each came back with the exact same attitude, and it was a turnaround from the season before. It's funny how it happened naturally without even talking about it.

"We just wanted to be happy. That was our goal. We just want to enjoy skating. We didn't want to be frustrated. We didn't want to feel bitter or disappointed. Both of us wanted to skate purely with the goal of being happy. We wanted to come off the ice every time we competed and feel good about what we had just done. It was so simple. Let's just be happy."

2014–2016: RIDING THE WINGS OF A QUAD TO THE TOP OF THE WORLD

Even though Meagan and Eric had yet to actually learn—let alone land—the throw quadruple Salchow, they set the choreography to fit the quad as the third element in the free skate. Then they set about learning it.

Meagan had always wanted to do it. She had landed two throw triple Axels with her first partner, Ryan. They had tried throw quad loops. One day the throw was so scary that Meagan and Ryan never did it again. But it was always something Meagan felt capable of doing. They would make Olympic history with this element in 2018, but saying you want to do a throw quadruple Salchow and actually doing it for the first time are two different things. Meagan remembers the process all too well.

"Some days we would practise the throw triple Salchow just for fun and tell our coaches, 'We're getting ready to do a quad.' "

Richard would disagree, telling them they would not do it, that Meagan could break her leg, that everybody who does a throw quad hurts themselves. Meagan was always adamant that she wouldn't hurt herself, that she had enough strength and body awareness.

"When the time came we thought we'd learn the throw quad starting with me in a harness just like a gymnast or diver learning advanced skills. When I tried one first as a throw double with the harness on me, it felt terrible and I hated it. It changed my timing and it didn't feel like my own throw anymore.

"Instead, we just tried the first throw quad cold turkey, on the ice. We skated around the rink, with me crapping my pants, saying, 'What the hell am I doing?' We set it up a few times and I chickened out, telling Eric no at the last second. Then we finally went for it.

"In the learning phase, sometimes we would go to set one up and then I would say, 'No, I'm not ready.' Or, I would freak right out; then we'd do another lap around the rink, go to set it up, and I would say, 'No, I'm not ready.' Then we'd do another lap while I was building up my courage."

Meagan knew that if her mind wasn't 100 per cent "there" for the quad, there was no point in even trying. She had to be fully committed to going for it or she would really hurt herself. Hence the so-called chickening out, that to non-skaters makes complete sense.

Even with complete mental commitment, the learning process was bloody and painful. Meagan didn't really wear any protective gear, but if she took a hard fall and wanted to continue practising quads, she would pack some sponge padding in her skating pants. She actually didn't wear much padding, and didn't wear it for long because she didn't want to rely on it. There wouldn't be a safety net when they competed, after all. She wore a little skating dress so she trained like she would be competing the quad.

She would leave the rink with huge hematomas on her butt and hip from the falls. Sitting down was difficult. Other times she could barely drive home after practice. She kept falling on the same spot on her hip every single day.

Meagan gave them seven weeks to learn the element and they did it in six. Every time out they drew closer to actually landing the element. She would glide a little longer before falling. Or her body would be more squared off and less twisted when she fell. Those were "good falls." Then she would step out. Then she would put a hand down. It was coming.

"The deadline was actually August 10, 2014, and it happened before that. I don't remember how many we tried that day before we landed it. But it had been in that progression phase. The day before we landed it cleanly, I put my hands down. It was inching closer and closer. But once we landed it, it was there."

There would be very few days in the final four years where they would not do a throw quad in practice. They would limit themselves, like it was a special treat. If they landed the first one or two then they didn't do any more. If the quad wasn't going well one day, they would work on a throw triple because it was safer.

They were deducted for falling so it was only worthwhile to include the quad if they could land it cleanly. Even a hand down would mean points deducted. At Worlds in 2015, Meagan put both hands down. Five teams earned more points with only throw triples.

The feeling was that Meagan and Eric won because of the quad; however, they believe they would have scored higher had they played it safe and just done a triple. While it wasn't true mathematically that they won with the throw quad, they were committed to the challenge of accomplishing it in competition. They were at that point in their skating where they were wondering what they could do next, and how they could continue to improve? How can they get from third position on the podium to the top?

They were skating boldly, aggressively, but with the calm acceptance that seemed to underscore all their great skates. They made some other changes, too. They told their coaches they weren't going to practise at 7:30 in the morning anymore. They would come for 8:30. On a grander scale, it's like they discovered who they were as skaters during the 2014–2015 season.

Working with Julie they developed a style and a system in their approach to their programs. It seemed to work best for them to create a short program with a lyrical, classical style. For the long program, they would switch it up to a new, modern rock style for the free skate. At the time, rock music was something pairs had never skated to before. And then there was the throw quadruple Salchow, the game-changer.

From the beginning Eric appreciated Meagan's cat-like ability to land any throw with anybody throwing her. But the throw quad seemed to be the limit. Eric's role may seem easier in the element than Meagan's, but Eric needed to be perfectly precise in order for Meagan to land the quad.

"My precision is exact. It was all in my arm placement. I have to pass Meagan, come behind her and then Meagan would launch. If I am even a mere two inches too wide, then Meagan would fall. There were times when Meagan would take off in the air, saying, 'Oh, shit.' She knew she wasn't placed perfectly."

On the throw Salchow, placement is key. Eric holds Meagan's arm with his left hand and her waist with his right. Some teams do the throw triple Salchow with both hands on the woman's waist, he explains, but Bruno had developed that slight variation, which seemed to make it easier to do a throw quad consistently, providing more stability for Meagan as she transferred from Eric's hand into the air on her own.

Eric stresses the importance of tracking and the positioning of each partner and how they relate to each other. When the quad worked well, the tracking was perfect. When they struggled with it, it was usually the tracking, and if not the tracking, then their timing was off.

"Doing a throw triple or a throw quad, I expend the same energy, regardless. I don't throw Meagan any higher or harder for one over the other; but for the quad, our accuracy and sensitivity are enhanced. For the most part, I knew if Meagan would land the throw as soon as she left my hands. Sometimes I would joke and wish her good luck. Obviously, I wanted her to land but it was more of a 'come on' when I released her.

"If it was a good one, there was a specific type of pressure in my left arm as the throw released. When Meagan left my hand, I would still feel pressure in my left hand until the very last second. There had to be no pressure moving side to side. It would feel like I was holding a weight with my left arm, but my arm held steady and didn't move. It was all very stable. A really good throw quad always felt like an elastic build up and a snap. For the most part I would know if it was going to be a good one."

But still, there was no accounting for the times when Eric thought they would miss the jump only to see Meagan land it on one foot. He would be left wondering how she had managed that. Then there were times when his throw was perfect and she missed the landing. That was always the most frustrating aspect of training—when everything felt great for one, but for some reason didn't work for the other.

After the Sochi Olympics, Meagan and Eric felt a release of pressure and expectation; with that came a real curiosity about what was going to come next. It was an interesting time as retirements and changes in teams had altered the skating landscape so the door was now

Meagan Duhamel and Eric Radford with Laura E. Young

open for a pairs team to come through and land on that top step, which seemed to have been reserved for the Germans and Russians. With those teams out of the picture came a new opportunity. Meagan and Eric had come third at Worlds in 2014, but there were still other talented teams behind them who had every opportunity to take that step up as well.

From a pure feeling of, "Let's just see what we can do," as opposed to worrying about what they had to do, Eric and Meagan were skating for themselves. They wondered where it would lead. Apparently, it was the pathway to success as their marks at competitions started to reflect their new mindset, and they were beating teams they never thought they would.

When they trained it was with a sense of freedom and of not really giving a damn about anything else, which allowed them to flourish. They experimented with different genres of music. Their choice of music by Muse in 2015 took them in a different direction from one any pair team had taken before. It was the first year the ISU allowed lyrics in the music and they were going to take full advantage of that.

But first, it was time to unleash the quad. Whenever they launched and landed the quad in competition it was so exciting because nobody had really ever seen it before. There was a great energy and anticipation around it. Word spread and people wanted to see it. Now they had the triple Lutz and a jump combination of triple toe, double toe, double toe to do, but these elements had become so consistent by then that the only real risk element was the throw quad. It did take a couple of trips out to get the throw quad consistent in competition, Meagan recalls.

"Early in the fall of 2014 we skated at our national team camp but the landings on the quad were a bit shaky. At the Autumn Classic we landed it for the first time on one foot in competition.

"Coming from a not-caring attitude, we took a big step in all areas of our skating that season. It wasn't just that we learned the throw quad and started landing it. Our lifts got better, the death spiral got better, the twist, our connection. It came not from trying harder but from relaxing more which may be the opposite of what people think athletes should do.

"And then we began to win. We may have talked about being on a winning streak, but only quietly to one another. 'How cool would it be if we won? We'd be undefeated this season.' It's like we didn't want to acknowledge it and let that thought creep into our heads, but it was something we definitely were aware of."

Throughout the entire season they trained clean short programs most of the time during practice. The side-by-side triple Lutz jump was extremely consistent and when they did a long program the only risky element was the quad, Eric remembers.

"That extreme consistency was different than we had experienced before. I remember skating around at practice, having an epiphany as the season went on. The elements felt easy and they seemed to flow one into another. I would skate and think, 'This is how a champion feels when they train.' "

That underlying quiet confidence was building during the season. The throw quad added to their confidence. Eric and Meagan had an undeniable skill, one that no one else had been able to master. Up until then, there was nothing like it in pairs skating. The points backed that up as well. They had a cushion of points with the triple Lutz, and now the throw quad in terms of base value.

They won Skate Canada and landed the throw quad at the Grand Prix Final. They were competing against Ksenia Stolbova and Fedor Klimov, the Olympic silver medallists from the individual event in Sochi, who were also winning everything and skating clean at every competition, Meagan remembers.

"And they were supposed to win. It was like we snuck up out of nowhere and we beat them. After our long program, we were sitting in the kiss and cry area with our coaches. We'd scored 146 points, which is a huge score. It took a couple of seconds and we thought, 'Wow, we just won the Grand Prix Final. It means we're the best in the world right now. This means we could win the World Championships.' We were in a whole other realm of skating.

"After we won the Grand Prix Final we took a moment to appreciate it. 'Wow, we're finished the first half of the season and we've won everything.' At the same time, the more important half of the season was coming up.

"Leading up to Worlds being undefeated was something new that we had to manage mentally. We were skating very well. Then our main Russian rivals pulled out of the World Championships. Everything was aligning and setting itself up for us to win the competition. It was a position we'd never been in before and it came with its own pressures and challenges."

For Eric, the ball of yes that comes with the perfect skate had returned to settle in his stomach as they waited their turn backstage at the 2015 Worlds.

"We were sitting backstage in our little nervous bubble. But during the whole season, we would talk about it with our sports psychologist and with each other, it was like a little ball of yes. There would be butterflies in your chest but a little ball of yes was solid in the gut, like a tiny, quiet voice that's whispering, 'Yes, yes, you can do it,' when you have all these doubts flying around in your head saying, 'No. You can't do it. This is impossible.' "

To add to all the pressure and excitement, it was one of those great nights for pairs skating, where everyone was skating a clean short program. Meagan and Eric were skating last so it was clear as day that they couldn't miss a thing in the short program or they would be completely out of the game. There was no room for error. The way it was going that night, they knew one mistake meant eighth place, if not lower.

They skated cleanly with a comfortable four-point buffer heading into the long program. They felt like all they had to do was maintain their energy instead of attacking the program. It would take a clean, though not necessarily perfect, long program to win it.

Then, the pressure was on for the night of the long program and Meagan and Eric did not start out as cleanly as possible. They landed the side-by-side Lutzes but the quad was a little messy and Eric slipped in the side-by-side spins. Eric reminded himself that he couldn't make any more errors.

"We came around the ice for our toe loop series, and the rest of the program ended well. We hit the ending position but it wasn't this big, magical moment as it had been a few months earlier, when we won the Grand Prix Final. It was okay, we had done our job. Then we had to wait. There were still two teams to skate after us."

Their main rivals, Sui Wenjing and Han Cong of China, sat just over four points back in third and skated last that night. They were landing every element. Eric wondered, "Oh, no. What if they score 150 points?"

Meagan was reassuring, "No, it's impossible. They skated clean all season and these are the marks they got."

The cameras came and focused on Eric and Meagan watching the marks appear. Eric's mind went blank, but as he would later recall, it all felt familiar.

"We had imagined this moment so many times, over and over again. Then it's really happening and it's hard to tell whether it's actually happening or if you're just imagining it again.

"All of a sudden we were world champions and for the rest of our lives, we would always be world champions. Even if we only won that one world title, nobody could take that from us. We had done it and it was an indescribable lifetime moment and achievement."

For Meagan, their undefeated season and the quadruple Salchow were having a snowball effect, the ball gaining momentum, with one thing creating the next wonderful moment, and the next.

"We kept going to competitions and skating clean. It was so easy. What made it so easy is hard to say. It's still a mystery. We were happy to win Skate Canada, the Grand Prix Final, and Canadians. Each competition had a special meaning to us. It all culminated at Worlds and it was amazing to win."

Eric and Meagan had spent their careers chasing a dream, as athletes do. At first, like all skaters, it was about lessons. Then it was moving away from home to train. There was the quest to learn the triple jumps. There was a sense that once they were paired they might also have been pursuing the skating world's respect as they pushed the technical envelope in their sport. After the 2014–2015 season, in which they won everything, including the World Championships, every goal they had pursued, seemed to be theirs.

What remained? The challenge became to keep pushing themselves, rather than becoming overconfident or even blasé in their success. Eric says they knew the other teams in the world would be gunning for them.

That thought brought the team into the next season. After winning Worlds they took a three-week break. Meagan and Bruno were officially married in Bermuda in June. Meagan and Eric toured in shows in Japan for most of the summer.

When they returned to Montreal, they began work on the Moulin Rouge short program for the 2015–2016 season. The music was powerful and made a real statement for the short program. For the long program they launched a musically contrasting free skate to "Hometown Glory" by Adele.

At the same time, they planned to evolve the throw quad and turn it into a throw Lutz. They had been practising it near the end of their tour and continued working on it through the summer.

The throw quad had become second nature and Eric and Meagan thought they had to change things up and push the technical difficulty even more. They thought everyone was going to learn the quad Salchow now because it seemed so easy to learn.

"Obviously, it wasn't easy, but we had learned it and incorporated it into competition more easily than anyone had ever done. We had landed it at almost every competition that year," Meagan reflects. "We thought we needed to add the quad Lutz. Maybe we took it for granted how impressive it was to learn the relatively easier Salchow and then consistently land it in competition. We assumed everybody else could and would do it.

"We had pushed the pairs bar, which needed to be done. For thirty years pairs skaters all did the same thing. They would do a triple twist, a side-by-side and throw triple Salchow. It was always the same. Literally in that order. We still see that, and if this was being done thirty years ago it shouldn't be the base anymore. The bar had to be set higher.

"That's what we did and we played to our strengths. We could do a side-by-side triple Lutz. Was it a risk? We probably missed our triple toe as much as we missed our triple Lutz. It came down to, if you're capable of doing something, why not do it? Why not try to push the sport in a direction that nobody had pushed it in so long?"

During that time, Eric began to notice a little spectre of self-expectation creeping into their thoughts. "When you win that first world title, you can tell yourself that you have it all figured it out and all you have to do is continue doing the same thing as before. But it doesn't work like that. Winning changes the direction of your focus, whether you like it or not. It's something that needs to be controlled, but since we'd never been in that position before, how did we know?

"You only know by making mistakes and having things go wrong. Then you can feel the difference between the way it was before and what's happening right now. Then you know how to get it back. And for us, that's really what happened."

They opened that season on the same foot they had left the 2014–15 season: undefeated. They won Skate Canada again and went to the 2015 Grand Prix Final in Barcelona undefeated. They had won everything for over a year. Once in Spain, there might have been a glimmer of worry, and thinking, "If you lose this, you lose the streak." For Eric, it wasn't something that made him nervous, the end of a streak, but he was also trying to convince himself that if they did lose, they had so much success behind them, it wouldn't be devastating.

They won Canadians in January for the fifth time. In February, they had a small hiccup at Four Continents in Taipei, Taiwan when Meagan was so sick the team could not compete. She vomited to the point of dehydration and could barely put one foot in front of the other to get to the bathroom. She was strongly encouraged to withdraw but eventually she did say that even if it were the Olympics, she couldn't skate. It would have been impossible to do a long program.

That season, they were training well but it was also frustrating because their solid training runs weren't carrying over to competition. As Eric recalls, they would step onto the ice and all their own expectations for themselves that hadn't been there before would begin to surface. Eric wondered if deep down they had started to fear losing, more so than they had in the previous season.

"We talk about skating for ourselves, but it's hard to put what that means into words. It's more of a feeling, of not caring what anyone else was thinking. For us, it was also about taking a leap of faith with the Muse music where we were making it our own, skating with that rough-around-the edges style that was ours, and being proud of making it our own. It also means that we were focused on ourselves. When we're not, we would hear what was going on around us, like hearing all the social media commentary. At an event it meant we were connected to the competition grapevine."

Then they would hear things like, "Oh, the judges are saying this about you." Or they would see another team trying a throw quad or something else incredible. Instead of ignoring it and focusing on themselves, it would distract them and pull their focus away from the event. Attention is energy. And, as Eric further explains, they were becoming more aware of what people were saying about the team on social media.

"The online commentary can make you second-guess yourself. People were posting all kinds of things, but it all boiled down to a common theme: 'How did they become world champions? They are the worst world champions I've ever seen.'

"We couldn't always ignore it. It was hurtful to read something that's mean about you, especially when you've worked your ass off and you're super passionate about skating. It really is part of you out there. Then somebody comes along and rips you to shreds.

"It's easy to say, 'Oh, you shouldn't read the comments.' But you're naturally curious. It was so hard not to scroll down a little bit. Then we'd read a comment and there you go. You're left with a bad thought or feeling by somebody anonymously writing something mean about you.

"When we're in our starting position on the ice, obviously we're not thinking about what people write about us online. But it lent itself to that slow growing self-expectation that we had started to put on ourselves that season that wasn't there in the 2014–2015 season."

Instead of letting things happen and letting the training take over, Meagan and Eric started to feel like they needed to prove to others and to themselves that they could still skate like world champions.

Despite all this, they stood on the ice in Boston in April and pulled the season together in a neat package, skating Adele's "Hometown Glory" perfectly to their second world title. Was this the time to retire?

SPOKESPERSONS AND OTHER CAUSES: COMING OUT AND VEGAN LIFE

Out and About

Eric Radford draws a deep breath as he settles in to reflect on his sexuality. It feels odd to have this conversation. I'm not having it with Meagan, after all.

In the years since Eric came out as gay in December 2014, post-Sochi Olympics, the world seems to be catching up and catching on.

In December 1998, Mark Tewksbury came out as Canada's first openly gay athlete. The 1992 Olympic champion in 100-metre backstroke promptly lost a six-figure contract as a motivational speaker.

But ultimately Tewksbury won: he served on a committee with the IOC, and was co-president of the Outgames in 2006 in Montreal, where he also raced. He is an award-winning LGBTQ educator, a TV commentator who delivers straight talk, and a not-to-be-missed motivational speaker.

Fellow Northern Ontario figure skater, Jeffrey Buttle, 2006 Olympic bronze medallist and 2008 world champion, married his partner, Justin Harris, in 2014. No one seemed to bat an eye, so is it really relevant to talk about people being gay, like it is a plot device for a movie?

Still, Eric remembers what it was like trying not to be gay.

"When I was thirteen and in Grade 9, Brian Orser was in the news for being gay. My music teacher asked me what I thought about this figure skater being gay. I had no clue. I didn't know what being gay was, back then. My mind wasn't there yet.

"But you know when you hit puberty, you start feeling sexual attraction. You begin to think, 'Oh, yeah, I find this attractive.' For the longest time I would feel so guilty about having those thoughts and feelings. I didn't want to accept them. I had promised myself I would never let myself be gay."

When Eric was fifteen, he started skating with coach Paul Wirtz, who was gay. Being around somebody like Paul, whom Eric admired and looked up to, and who taught the skater so much, made Eric feel more comfortable.

When Eric was eighteen or nineteen, he went to an event with a friend who introduced him to Mark Tewksbury. By that time Eric knew Mark's compelling story and had accepted being gay, although Eric was not out.

"Mark said to me, 'Wow, you could be a great poster child for gay athletes in the future.' I remember thinking that would be so cool, but I was very young at the time and I had never done anything in skating. I didn't really think about it that much after that."

By the Olympic Games in Sochi 2014, Eric was a three-time Canadian champion and a world bronze medallist. He had achieved something in sport. Before the Olympic Games in Sochi he was contacted by GLAD (GLBTQ Legal Advocates & Defenders), who hoped he would come out before the games or at the games. It left Eric feeling uncomfortable.

"One day, I was driving home and had parked outside my house. I had just gotten off the phone with GLAD. At that point I thought maybe I really could make a difference if I told my story at the right time. It could have a lot of impact and maybe that was the best way to go about it. When I got off the phone with GLAD, I called my parents and told them what I had decided to do.

"You know, you think you have a good idea, then you say it to somebody. They're quiet and don't say anything. That's how my parents reacted. Neither one of them said anything at first. Then they told me that they didn't think it was a good idea to go to the Olympics and tell everyone I was gay. The idea of my saying something before heading to Russia scared them. Russia was passing all these anti-LGBTQ laws. They were worried for my safety. I think they were just worried for me in general.

"I remember when I hung up after speaking with my parents. I don't know why but I felt so upset and I started crying. I felt like a coward, like I had given in to the fear of not being true to myself and not doing the courageous and more difficult thing."

Leading up to the Olympics in Sochi, Eric and his publicist had a plan: if the opportunity presented itself, then maybe Eric would go for it and make the announcement. If not, then it was fine and nothing was lost.

For Eric, the main priority was obvious—go to Sochi and concentrate on what he needed to do. It was his first Olympics and he wanted it to be about himself and his Olympic experience. It wasn't supposed to be about this other part of his life. Canada won the team event silver medal. He wondered whether this could be his moment.

There was a flurry of statements from athletes and media attention focused on LGBTQ Olympians in Sochi, such as married couple Cheryl Maas of the Netherlands and Stine Brun Kjeldaas from Norway. After competing in snowboard, Maas drew attention for waving her rainbow mitten at the television cameras to show her support of LGBTQ people in Russia. The media attention surprised Eric.

"I couldn't believe how fast these stories were happening. I realized I could come out, but maybe ten or fifteen minutes later, somebody else would win a medal and something else would happen. My coming out would just pass by and it wouldn't be effective. It would be lost in everything else that was happening, which was another reason it seemed like it wasn't the right time."

Still, Eric did want to go public for a combination of reasons, if the opportunity presented itself at some point. He was at a stage in his life and career where any sort of fear, doubt or reason that may have previously held him back was not as important anymore. And, after an excellent 2013–2014 season, two world bronze medals and an Olympic silver medal, Eric felt like his voice was perhaps strong enough now, should he decide to officially come out that season.

He had a friend who was on the Canadian Olympic Committee and part of the One Team Initiative, a partnership of organizations working to create a more LGBTQ inclusive environment in sports. Eric thought it was a very important program, and was told he'd be a great fit. His friend at the COC planted the seed in Eric's head about coming out and the difference doing so could make. He also put Eric in touch with somebody who could tell Eric's story when and if he wanted to do it.

"Then there was a personal reason of just what I went through when I was younger, growing up in a small town, being a figure skater, getting bullied—there were not many openly gay figure skaters, hardly any openly gay athletes. It would have made a big difference to me, having somebody like myself to look up to. I just felt like I could make a difference.

"In December 2014 I came out through an interview in *Outsports*. The day it hit the stands, I went to the gym full of anxiety and panic, thinking maybe I shouldn't have done this. I thought that maybe I shouldn't have said anything, that it would have been so much easier, that I wouldn't have all this stress.

"When you're worried or fearful about something, you can blow reality out of proportion. You create these scenarios that probably aren't true at all. What if I'm losing possible opportunities by being open about my sexuality when I don't really need to be?"

Then Eric's cell phone started ringing, almost off the table. Skate Canada was calling because reporters wanted to talk to him. There were emails and texts from different journalists.

Two days later, Eric was in the village in Montreal. He went to a convenience store and there on the front page of the *National Post* was his photo, up in the corner: "Figure Skater Eric Radford hopes coming out 'can make a difference'." He bought a copy and found a lengthy article.

It's not that this news was surprising, Eric reflects. Another male figure skater comes out as gay. And it was hardly news that there are stereotypes about male figure skaters and their sexuality, which are not true, he adds. Eric had figured maybe the gay communities in North America and some dedicated skating fans who dig into that stuff on figure skating would find the news in *Outsports*. He didn't think it would be a front-page story but was happy it was being taken seriously.

In the proceeding weeks Eric was inundated with messages from people around the world who just wanted to say thank you and let him know that his story was so inspiring. Young high school and college athletes from the U.S. thanked him for telling his story. He heard from people who knew they were gay but weren't out. Yet some were older gay men who told Eric that he was setting a good example.

"After I came out, we went to the Grand Prix Final in Barcelona. We were on a practice session with the Russians. Dylan came up to me and said, 'One of the Russian skaters asked me if all the guys on the Canadian team are gay now.'

"Dylan said, 'Ah, no.'

"We don't know if the Russian was joking, but when Dylan told me, I felt uncomfortable that they would say something like that. We were sharing a dressing room with the Russians. The other teams were finishing when I walked in; there were six of them changing. They were laughing but when I walked in and they saw me, the room went silent. It brought me right back to being in school—that horrible, awkward, bad feeling, very uncomfortable. I went in, got my stuff and left. They didn't say a word. They were silent the whole time.

"It was only uncomfortable for one of the practices and then I let it go and didn't worry about it. There was nothing I could do about it anyway, even though it shook me up a little bit."

Naturally there were anonymous, snarky swipes online: "Oh a figure skater is gay, how surprising." After Eric and Meagan won the Grand Prix Final and beat a Russian team who were favoured to win, Eric read comments on YouTube that said maybe the Russian skater should pretend to be gay so he would score higher component marks. But Eric laughs about it. The world's reception of his news had been overwhelmingly positive.

"Of course, there's always going to be bullying of young LGBTQ people and athletes. When I talk to any male in figure skating, I realize we were all bullied in school. Not badly, but we all get made fun of because, as we're told, it's a 'girls' sport.' It's unfortunate, but I don't know how you stop it, because kids say what they want to say. That's just the way it's going to be.

"But I do think there has been a big change in sports. You're starting to see athletes in professional sports come out after they've retired. At least it opens people's minds to the fact that there are gay athletes in professional sports. Just because you don't know they are there, doesn't mean they aren't. Personally, I don't think people really care; they just want them to score a goal.

"As people come out, it will slowly desensitize people to the fact that there are gay people in all areas of life, including sport. It will become a smaller, less surprising issue. Then, for the general public, it will become old news.

"Let's say I didn't come out publicly, and I put a picture of me proposing to my boyfriend on Instagram and that's all there was to it. People would know. People who already knew would be really happy for me. That's the direction I feel we're heading towards on same-sex lifestyles."

After coming out, Eric felt an invisible weight lift off his shoulders. He noticed his skating became more expressive, and he had a new what-the-hell-attitude that really helped Meagan and Eric compete in 2014–2015. They skated a clean short program at every competition and made perhaps one error in the long program. Eric's coming out tied into that season's theme of letting go and skating for themselves.

Meagan Walked Into a Bookstore and Walked Out a Vegan

In judged sports where an ideal body image battles with the reality of one's body and the need to feed it, Meagan found a way to make her body type work. She accepted early on that she wasn't going to look like all the other skaters.

Skating junior ladies, Meagan was always short and small but stocky in a way female skaters normally were not. She doesn't remember it ever really bothering her as a teenager. That's just the way she was. It didn't cause internal issues. She remembers just accepting that her build was another thing that made her different, but it didn't mean that it was wrong. By skating standards, she may have always been a little bigger than many of her competitors, but she could always do what she needed to do.

"Sometimes I was insecure about it and I'd try to change my workouts thinking I could make my legs smaller or something like that. It didn't matter if I lost weight; I was still going to be muscular. I don't have to do any strength training; I'm going to be muscular. There's nothing I can do about that. At the end of the day your body is your body. I accepted long ago that's how it was going to be and that I would make the most of what my body can do."

Meagan accepts that in skating, everyone is judged, and outfits or costumes are usually sleeveless and show a lot of back and legs. When planning outfits for competition, they always worked with designs that made Meagan look as slim and as tall as possible. It's always been like that: considering whether a certain cut of material makes her shoulders look bigger than they are, or if her waist looks more square than it is. Clothes aren't going to cover that much.

Meagan was never caught up in thinking "Oh, dear. I have sheer fabric on my stomach and everybody can see my stomach." She feels proud of her body and happy that she has a strong stomach and core supporting her. She's also proud to have strong legs. That means she can do a throw quad.

Meagan noticed a trend as she got older. She'd gain a little bit of weight, or was out of shape in the spring or summer, and then a coach would say, "Oh, how are your off-ice gym workouts going?"

"In 2007, when I first moved to Montreal, I wore a skating dress to practice one day. A coach told me, 'Um, that dress makes you look fat. You shouldn't wear that anymore.'

I couldn't believe anyone would actually open their mouth and say that so bluntly. I was really insulted but I was also twenty-one years old so I was sure of myself. It didn't cause psychological problems. It flashed off me. I know this is my body and there's nothing I can do about it. I just couldn't believe someone would say that out loud."

Up until that point, Meagan's diet was pretty standard, but in retrospect, she wouldn't say she had a well-rounded diet. The Duhamels never were big meat eaters growing up. Meagan thinks she's only had steak once in her life. Her family ate a lot of fish. Later, when she was living on her own, she couldn't cook well. Every now and then she thought she should probably eat some protein. She'd go out and get a chicken or a turkey sub sandwich.

Some mornings she'd pick up a juice box and a granola bar for breakfast at the gas station. The "meal" would cost one dollar. She remembers eating a lot of granola bars and bananas when she didn't have much money. She would buy a bagel at Tim Hortons. It was convenient and cheap. She also ate a lot of Subway and Quiznos.

In 2008, Meagan was travelling and was browsing through the airport bookstore for something to read. She happened on a book about the vegan lifestyle, called *Skinny Bitch* by Rory Freedman and Kim Barnouin. It could be said that Meagan walked into the bookstore and became a vegan, but at the time she didn't think of it as a life-changing moment.

"I thought the book looked funny and like something I would read. I knew about vegetarians and people who had lactose allergies but I had never met a vegan or heard that something like this even existed until I read the book. The book wasn't profoundly enlightening but the authors were funny and they made the story engaging. I read it in one shot and thought, 'Oh, that seems like something I should try.'

"I went cold turkey. I didn't think anything of it and I actually didn't think it would be that hard to do. I didn't know much back then. It was more that I was thinking how cool it was and fun, even. I was going to try it.

"I threw everything out of my fridge and made my coffee the next day. Maybe I should have bought soy milk before I did the purge because then I realized I had no milk to put in my coffee. I thought, 'I guess I drink black coffee now.'"

She learned by scouring the Internet because she couldn't afford to buy many books. Eventually she bought books or would receive them as gifts. She learned to read labels carefully. It was trial and error at first. She learned her vitamins and minerals, and the nutritional density of the food she was eating. She started to feel really good and developed a passion for healthy living. In 2010, she began studying holistic nutrition, converting to a more natural, organic way of life all around, not just with her food. And she felt better and better about herself the deeper she dove into it.

She was eating more nutritionally dense food and avoiding the fast food outlets. She lost between five and ten pounds which was a lot for her frame. Her weight remained stable. She doesn't count her calories. When she's hungry, she eats. She doesn't limit anything because, as she says, what she puts in her body is the right type of food and it's all serving a purpose. But she has a sweet tooth, and truly likes her desserts.

In the beginning it was harder to travel and eat nutritiously. But today, there are vegan and organic restaurants and grocery stores everywhere they go in the world. It's much easier now than it would have been twenty years ago, though she does carry the necessities because she doesn't want to be stuck. She says sometimes it's better to rest at a competition than sit in a taxi or a subway station for two hours a day trying to get food.

"I don't think everyone needs to be a vegan, but people need to be healthy. Holistic nutrition is not just studying being a vegan. It's about the best whole, organic foods, the best quality of food and nutritional density.

"For me, being a vegan is a lifestyle, not just a diet because it transfers over into everything in my life. It may have started out as a diet but it became a lifestyle. It became part of me and a catalyst to other things in my life.

"I wouldn't say being vegan has made me more patient with my skating but I do think my compassion and patience off-ice were enhanced. I don't know if it improved or I just became more aware of that side of me. I'm not sure you just innately develop a new trait. I think it was brought to the surface a little bit more. You're not putting fear and anger into your body anymore."

Meagan doesn't know if she would have adopted her dogs, though, if she hadn't changed her lifestyle and become vegan. She rescued a twelve-year-old Jack Russell terrier from the SPCA in 2008, after she'd first moved to Montreal and before becoming a vegan. It was her second year in Montreal and skating was getting stressful.

Kaiser was a great companion to Meagan, but unfortunately, Meagan's packed schedule and living alone made it difficult to care for a dog. She didn't have the luxury of being able to afford to pay a dog walker like she does now. Her parents took Kaiser about a year after Meagan adopted him. He ended up living to be nineteen years old. He was put down in 2016.

In 2014, Meagan and Bruno went to Ottawa and rescued a beagle, Theo. They had tests done to see what type of dog matched their personalities. Meagan learned that beagles are one of the dogs used to test drugs, make-up, cleaning products and nicotine, to name a few. She feels science has advanced enough that animal testing is unnecessary, now.

She supports the Rescue & Freedom Project, as well as Free Korean Dogs. She would not have found those organizations if she hadn't been passionate about the vegan lifestyle.

Meagan would like to get a beagle that was rescued from a lab, but her condo is too small. One day, she says, she'll live on a farm and have an animal sanctuary with space for all of them.

"Becoming a vegan also gave me direction for my future, after we retire from competitive skating. I want to use my foundation in holistic nutrition and create a wellness program for athletes now that I'm finished competing and when my sports and fitness nutrition degree is done. I want to teach other people well-being, living a holistic lifestyle as an elite athlete.

"There's so much emphasis on just going to the gym and going to the rink and doing your training when a lot of other things like nutrition and mental training, regular therapy and treatment to maintain your body gets pushed to the side. Yet it's just as important as a training session, which I'm not sure a lot of athletes realize. I think this is the direction the elite sporting world is going, and needs to go, to sustain the extreme things athletes are doing now. The body can deal with a lot if you take care of it and give it the right platform."

Without following a vegan lifestyle Meagan doesn't think she would have studied holistic nutrition. She wouldn't have learned how to fuel her body properly, in a way that allowed her to recover at the rate she did when she was competing at the highest levels. That rate was much faster than anyone she had trained with, and Meagan believes it had to do with what she was putting in her body. It seemed that was the only thing she was doing differently than others.

The vegan lifestyle led Meagan to make healthier decisions around how she takes care of herself and her body, which gave her career longevity, she believes. She expects that if she hadn't made these changes, she'd still be skating, but wouldn't be as healthy as she is. She thinks it's "pretty remarkable" that at thirty-two years old she was doing quads, triple Lutzes and triple twists and had not had a serious injury in eight years.

Ultimately Meagan didn't want to be like anybody else. She always wanted to do things differently and stand out. Perhaps that's why her size and shape never bothered her. She would see the pressure on people to look a certain way and always wondered why people cared so much. She says, "If you feel good, you can do everything you need to do and you feel like you're living to your potential and always improving—shouldn't that be enough?

"Besides, if being stick thin and having no shape is what people are going to consider beautiful, that's not what I want to be. That wouldn't be natural to me. Why would anybody want to be something other than just who they are?

"I can't speak for other sports but when I think about Canadian skaters, the best female skaters we've had—Joannie Rochette, Kaetlyn Osmond and Gabrielle Daleman—they're all strong and powerful. It's the same for all the female partners in pairs that have been successful for Canada.

"I don't know why but in general Canadians seem to embrace who we are. Kaetlyn doesn't look like the Russian girls but having the strength she does gives her enormous jumps, and huge speed and power across the ice that some other skaters can't have. It's give or take, which one do you want? At the end of the day, you work with your strengths."

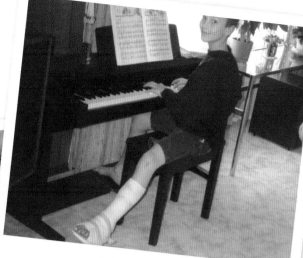

PIANO MAN:
The piano has always been there – even when a gymnastics injury at age 9 took him out for a time

SUPER CYCLE:
During their time in Imbil, Australia, Rick Radford fixed two used bikes for Richard and Eric

CORE SPORT:
Gymnastics played a key role in Eric's sporting development

NORTHERN ONTARIO CLASSIC:
Fishing and the lake were always part of the Radford family lifestyle

MOM, I'M HOME

STRIKE THE POSE:
Eric was the only male skater in his hometown

BROTHERS 2014:
Eric and Richard share a moment at
the Sochi Olympics

CHRISTMAS 2017:
Three generations of Radfords select their Christmas
tree, (from left) Taylor, Rick, Eric, Wendy, Valerie, & RJ.

JUST LIKE UNCLE ERIC:
Taylor warms up with her uncle and Grandpa R

A STREET WITH HIS NAME:
Balmertown celebrates its Olympic Champion with Eric Radford Way

RADFORDS 2018:
Rick, Eric, Richard, and Valerie in PeyongChang

BRING ON THE CUPCAKES:
Balmertown ensured everyone got a taste of their newest street

LIFEMATES:
Eric and Luis Fenero announced their engagement in 2017

MEET THE PARENTS:
Eric, Luis, Valerie, Rick, and Luis' parents Maria Luisa Bisquer, & Jose Antonio Fenero visit Niagara Falls

OTHER PASSIONS:
Meagan's love of four-legged friends blossomed to supporting various charities and issues for the ethical care of animals

MOM AND ME:
Heidi with her happy middle child

FIRST LESSON:
In 1988, Meagan took her first trip around the ice in Lively

WE ARE FAMILY:
Meagan, Johnny and Heather Duhamel lived up the road from Lively's indoor and outdoor rinks

WALL OF FAME:
Meagan never dreamed that three Olympic medal would one day join the hardware from her early days in skating

HOMETOWN JOY:
Nancy Tuominen was a dedicated supporter of Meagan's career, long before she celebrated Meagan's team silver medal from Sochi

STRIKE THE POSE:
Eventually Meagan would choose the show and sport of skating from a long list of activities

SIBS IN SOCHI:
Meagan, Johnny, and Heather share some down time at the 2014 Olympics

DO YOU BELIEVE WE'RE AT THE OLYMPICS?
In 2014 Heidi and Danny joined Meagan in Sochi

THREE GENERATIONS:
Heidi Duhamel, her mom Raili Koski, and Meagan
celebrate Meagan's homecoming in June 2018

A STREET WITH HER NAME:
Meagan and her uncle Kevin ensure the sign
is well secured in August 2018

LET THERE BE CAKE:
In June 2018 the celebrations of Meagan's career
included cake at her high school in Lively

OLYMPIC GRADUATE:
Lively High principal Leslie Mantle gave Meagan
a high school graduation ceremony, June 2018

BY MY SIDE:
Meagan and Bruno celebrated their accomplishments and a new phase of their lives together in Lively in June 2018

BE OLYMPIC:
In winning the 2012 Canadians Eric and Meagan first realized they could be Olympians

AVERAGE NORTHERN ONTARIO KIDS:
Friends off the ice, Eric and Meagan take the snowmachine for a spin

CLASSIC PAIRS:
Meagan and Eric perform their death spiral in their short program at the 2017 Worlds

2018 OLYMPIC PAIRS PODIUM:
(From Left) China's Wenjing Sui and Han Cong,
Germany's Aljona Savchenko and Bruno Massot, and
Canada's Meagan and Eric

FAMILY SUPPORTERS
Duhamels and Radfords celebrate the
2018 Olympic medallists

TRIPLE TWIST:
Meagan and Eric's performances were instrumental
in Canada claiming Olympic gold team event
in PyeongChang

RESPECT:
Eric, Aljona, Meagan, and Bruno celebrate a
night to remember in Olympic pairs skating

2016–2017: IF I LOSE, AM I A LOSER?

As athletes know all too well, the third of anything is the toughest. It doesn't matter at what level the athlete toils. There isn't a weekend warrior masters swimmer who doesn't hurt badly in the third 100-metres of the 400-metre freestyle. The third year, the one before the Olympic season, elite athletes suffer like the damned where they rest in a harbour of doubt. How can they go through this? It's still not even the Olympics yet.

Meagan and Eric's rise in figure skating had been steadily upward, so perhaps they were due for an off season. But in the 2016-17 season something else was off between the teammates, and it peaked with injuries at the 2017 World Championships.

Eric reflects on the rarity of a winning streak. There are always individual moments but to have a season undefeated in the world of figure skating, indeed, of any sport, was an incredible achievement.

"I was speaking with Kaitlyn Weaver. That season she and Andrew Poje were undefeated in ice dance until Worlds. She said to me, 'Don't you just miss those days where it was like, 'Oh, we won another one. Oh, we won another one. It just seemed so easy.'

"I said, 'I know. It just seemed like it was all meant to happen back then.'"

Eric and Meagan did not retire after winning their second world title in Boston because they were halfway through the Olympic quadrennial. They had won twice. Everything was falling into place leading up to the ultimate goal of winning a medal at the Olympics. The 2016–2017 season meant they were even closer to the 2018 Olympics, so what was one more year? When they were at the Sochi Olympics they both knew they wanted to experience the excitement again.

On a practical level, they had not begun to prepare for life after skating. Had they stopped, the change would have been too abrupt. They would have found themselves very much lost in their own lives.

Then there was the matter of improvement. It's like any sport. One can always try to run faster, jump higher. It feels like there is more to give, more to achieve. But as Eric reflects, having that success two years in a row did change something fundamentally for him as he and Meagan headed into the next season.

"At first, it seemed like my body was fine and ready to compete. There were the usual aches and pains. Every once in a while, my shoulder would start to hurt, or my knee would start to hurt. I was still learning how my body was feeling as it was aging in skating. I would feel an ache and think, 'Oh, no. What is this? How long is it going to be until this is normal? Is this going to keep me off the ice?' "

One morning, while Meagan and Eric were on tour in Japan, Eric noticed a little click in his shoulder that hadn't been there the night before. While he was learning there were sometimes just natural aches and pains, he thought he had torn his rotator cuff. He was going to need surgery. Should he have the surgery as soon as possible or should he wait? He had a mini anxiety attack over it, but over time he learned that with exercise and physio, and if he took better care of himself, the pain would go. And it did.

When it came time to designing the programs for the 2016–2017 season, Julie suggested Meagan and Eric could try skating to "Killer" by Seal. Eric says it was a little bit more of a risk in terms of music choice, but they had already won twice and had already skated to two pop artists, Coldplay and Adele, for their long programs. Sure, let's just try something new, they thought.

"For the first time ever in our careers, the judges who came to watch us practise our programs and give us feedback told us, 'Meagan, you look great. Eric, you look like you're struggling. You're out of place. Your energy doesn't match the music.'

"That type of really upbeat, smile-smile-smile performance is not me at all. I figured I could act fairly well but I don't think it ever came across as well as we would have hoped because it's not in my soul."

When Eric looks back at their long program that season, skating to "Non, je ne regrette rien," he finds it interesting that on one level the program worked. The music was nice. It had intensity. It had ups and downs. But for some reason the program as a whole never connected. He doesn't know whether it was the choreography or the order of elements. It might well have been that he and Meagan didn't effectively hit the highlights of the music. After the Muse program, which was really bombastic, and the Hometown Glory program, which was emotional, the "Non, je ne regrette rien," program never really resonated.

For Eric, the wheels began to fall off early in the season, even though at first it seemed like he and Meagan would pick up where they had left off. Their first event was Patinage Quebec's Souvenir Georges Éthier—a local event entered to get the programs out on the ice. They skated cleanly and scored 152 points for the long program. Once again, it seemed like everything was going to be so easy.

Still, Eric remembers something was changing. In mid-October they were heading to Finlandia Trophy while Eric was working on a musical project with his friend, Elad Simhony. They had started compiling songs for an album Eric wanted to release. Working on music was so invigorating and stimulating in a new, exciting way. And that fulfilment off-ice, combined with going into another season after they had won twice, left Eric feeling lost for the first time.

He wondered about his goals in skating. There are always the typical goals: skate clean. Obviously. Then, win Worlds again. But the drive to win didn't hold the same excitement and spark it once did. Now there was another season before the Olympics. It was almost as though Eric was running out of motivational steam.

"When I went into the rink, as opposed to feeling present and aware, and really driven towards a goal, I began to feel like I was going through the motions. I would still land my jumps; we would do throw quads. Before, when we were winning, we would land it, and I'd think, 'Wow, that means we're going to be world champions and win first place.' Now the purpose behind it all wasn't the same as it had been. Skating started to feel more like work rather than the fun sport I had always wanted to explore and see just how far it would take me."

Skate Canada in October was better, and they landed the throw triple Axel in the short program for the first time in competition, which created a lot of buzz. The long program was decent enough. They won the NHK Trophy in Japan, but missed the Lutzes and the throw Axel with a hard fall. The same thing happened in the Grand Prix Final; they placed third.

Part of the frustration lay in the fact they were training well, only to skate poorly in competition. A feeling of discouragement was building within Eric. There they were, putting in so much time and training, only to have nothing to show for it. They would land amazing throw triple Axels in practice, and then, as Eric recalls, when they actually needed to land it, the throw didn't work.

Eric was left disheartened in a way failure hadn't affected him before. In practice and in training he was doing everything he needed to do, but it all felt a little deflated. The main question Eric kept returning to was, Why was he doing this? Why wasn't there much enjoyment and fulfilment—even in the successes?' Did he need to win another world title to be happy? No, he felt so complete.

"I don't know if I had become jaded or if I was starting to see other teams get better while we kept making mistakes. Maybe it was a defense mechanism: I wouldn't let myself get worked up because I didn't want to feel let down when we didn't win. I wondered if the best times were behind us. I thought about all this. I'd meditate and do some soul-searching. But my brain couldn't change the way my heart was feeling.

"Periodically we worked with a sports psychologist, but I felt I couldn't voice these feelings to anybody. In fact, it made me feel a little stupid. What am I going to tell somebody? 'Oh, I just don't feel motivated?' Everybody has times where they don't feel motivated. Here I am doing the sport that I love and it's afforded me all those amazing moments and things in my life and I'm going to be whining that I'm not motivated.

Meagan Duhamel and Eric Radford with Laura E. Young

"Life has its ebbs and flows. We had been on a high for so long and had won pretty much everything. You do see skaters win one year and then they can't seem to hit their stride the next season. You wonder what changed. Maybe they don't even know themselves."

It was time for Meagan and Eric to endure that third-year struggle. Eric could logically think of all the reasons why it was happening, but knowing and understanding the reasons didn't change his lack of motivation at the thought of going to the rink or to the next competition. Away from the rink, he was drawn to work on his music, and excited about the different projects coming up in his life in music.

On the ice, his jumps were off, and he started having problems with his triple Lutz. It became less reliable and that trouble shook his confidence. The side-by-side jump had been their go-to staple element in their technical repertoire and now it was becoming a risky element. His hip was starting to hurt more and more. It may well have been partly physical and partly that his technique was off and never really came back the same way.

About three weeks before the Four Continents event in PyeongChang, Korea, Eric began waking up in the morning unable to bend forward. He was having trouble putting on his socks and shoes. His back was in spasm, but it would warm up as he started skating.

On the ice, folding down into the piked position on the side-by-side spins was the only thing that really hurt Eric's back. It changed the way he had to do that one element. But for the most part he was able to train every day and it didn't seem like the spasms were affecting him too badly. Yet.

Before they left for Finland and the 2017 Worlds, Eric wound up with a bad cough. At times he coughed so hard he couldn't catch his breath. He'd almost throw up. They were driving to do a show in Quebec City and the combination of sitting in his car and coughing severely aggravated his back. After the show his back was in pain, but again he was still able to do everything he needed to do.

The ISU World Figure Skating Championships were held in Helsinki at the end of March 2017. Eric and Meagan skated well in the first practice. Massages seemed to give Eric some relief, but not much. After the first practice at Worlds, Eric and Meagan walked to a restaurant for dinner. The muscles in and around Eric's hip began to feel quite tight. He couldn't find a comfortable sitting position as they waited for their meal. He couldn't be sure if it was his back or his hip. They took a cab back to the hotel.

"When I woke up the next morning something felt weird. My back hurt so badly and when I went to lift my leg, the muscle was so flexed it wouldn't respond. At practice, I could barely skate basic crosscuts. When I tried to lift my leg it felt like it was made of wood. It took all my willpower not to have a full-blown panic attack. I thought, 'Okay, I just need to relax my mind. My body can do this.'"

At practice, Eric managed to complete a triple toe jump but his legs felt like they wanted to fly apart in the air. His adductor muscle wasn't firing either. When it came to the triple Lutz, his legs were definitely flying apart in the air. He could not do it—no matter how much he concentrated, there was no hope. He told their coaches, "I don't know what I'm going to do." Bruno and Richard kept saying, "Just relax. Get some therapy. You have your other practice this evening. We'll deal with it then."

The night of their next practice, Eric warmed up, struggling to activate his leg muscle. Eventually he was able to jump the Salchow and the toe loop, and for the first ten minutes of the practice, his muscles seemed to be firing a little bit better. Then they got tired really fast and when the time came to do the Lutz, Eric felt like he was killing himself. He would fly in the air and only complete two-and-a-half rotations before landing on his back.

Eric went over to the boards to talk to Richard, who told him to concentrate and try to push through the pain. Eric tried to explain, saying, "Listen. I cannot squeeze my legs together. There's something wrong in my hip." At the time Eric thought the problem was in the hip. He didn't realize it was coming from his spine.

His coach said, "Go and do one more triple Lutz, and if it doesn't work, then you'll have to withdraw."

"I remember thinking, 'I can do a Salchow and a toe jump. Maybe it's possible to do a side-by-side-triple toe loop instead of our usual Lutz, even though Meagan hasn't even tried one in a couple of months because it would hurt her foot.' All I knew was the Lutz wasn't going to work and I started to think we were going to have to withdraw.

"Bruno sat down with me and said, 'Listen, we can put a toe jump in tomorrow. You can do this. You're going to get through the short.' He really calmed me down."

But that night Eric's anxiety returned. He couldn't sleep and called Julie back in Montreal. She helped Eric weigh his options and come up with a plan of action for the next day.

They were practising the next day when Meagan overheard Richard and Bruno saying that if Eric didn't do the triple, they would have to withdraw. She scooted to Eric and said, "The Lutz isn't going to work, let's do the toe loop."

He thanked her.

Their music was going to be played next in the practice rotation. They chose a little pattern so they could flow into the toe loop jump. The entry into the triple toe jump was on the same pattern as the Lutz. A Salchow would have changed their choreography and since they were competing that night, there was no time to make a change. They switched to the triple toe. Meagan tried her first triple in three months once and then their music played.

Their names were called, they went and did it. It all happened within one minute. The decision was made; they put in a toe jump and did it in practice. Now they felt confident they could do it in competition.

When the time came to compete in the short program, Meagan and Eric made it through relatively well, despite a bobble on the throw Lutz. They were a little disappointed to be ranked seventh, but for Eric it was a miracle he was able to skate at all.

The next day they practised before the long program. Again, for the first five or ten minutes, Eric's hip felt like it was reacting properly. Then it felt as though the muscle just gave out as soon as the music started. His leg wouldn't fire or move. At this point, even a crosscut was really hard—a basic skating element. He certainly couldn't do a flying camel spin. He didn't even know if he would be able to rotate at all in their jumps. He was starting to wonder, "How am I going to do this? Can I do this and is it safe to do this?"

"In pairs skating if we're going to have an accident, the male partner's goal is to save the girl, basically. But now I just didn't know. If we put up a lift, would I trip and fall with my leg not moving properly? What if something really bad happened and I knew I shouldn't have been skating in the first place? That gave me a lot of anxiety and when we got off the ice after practice, I was very emotional and upset.

"I was really on the cusp of giving up. I called my sports psychologist in Canada. He said I should go out and at least try. When I got to the rink, I remember going up and seeing my parents. My mother held it together really well. She could see I was upset. I was crying. I told her I didn't think I could do it. 'I don't think it's worth it to go out there and skate for a minute, then have to stop. It would be so embarrassing.'"

In that moment Eric decided he couldn't skate. He went downstairs to rink level in the elevator. He was crying as he headed into the skaters' lounge. He could see people looking at him, wondering why he was so upset. He sat down with Bruno, Meagan and Mike Slipchuk, the team leader, and told them he didn't think he could skate. "I'm worried about Meagan's safety," he said. He was overwhelmed.

As they sat, Bruno began reassuring Eric, saying, "I believe you can go out there and get through. If you can't, then it's okay, but you will have given it everything you had." Then he asked the million-dollar question: "If this was the Olympics, what would you do?"

Of course, Eric said, "I would go out and try."

"But in my mind, it wasn't the same thing. The Olympics are the end of the road. There was still something beyond this World Championships, like the Olympic season. I was also worried I might make whatever was wrong with me even worse. I wasn't quite sure exactly what my injury was at that time."

But in the end, Bruno injected enough confidence in Eric to go for it. Eric thought he and Meagan did a decent job on the free skate. They did the jumps. The first lift was the tricky reverse lasso, a technically difficult lift because Meagan would fly backwards up and over Eric's head while doing a full turn on the way up. Then they catch and they end up on opposite arms, Meagan on the right, Eric on the left. She grabs her leg.

Fortunately, it was the first lift in the program, so Eric wasn't that tired. He actually managed the lift better than he thought he would. He was more worried about the second lasso lift later in the program where he takes off in a spreadeagle position with his legs open. It had been a difficult element for Eric to do in Finland. But somehow, he was able to move his oddly numb leg enough to get everything done in the free skate.

He never felt like he was going to drop Meagan, but he could feel his leg lagging on the turns in their lifts. Usually their lifts soar down the ice, but not this time, because his leg wasn't responding the way it normally did. Eric deliberately took extra time with them, though, trying to be more patient and cautious so he could get the job done even though it was sloppy. They had a fall on the throw quad but Eric was just happy he'd completed all three lifts and hadn't seriously injured Meagan in the process. He managed to get through the side-by-side spin. He was genuinely proud of himself. It would be the most difficult skate of his entire career.

"Some commentators acted like we'd had this big fall from grace, saying things like, "They were once world champions and now they're in seventh place." I was so proud that I went out there and made it through. I could barely move.

"Not only did we come seventh in the world, we secured the maximum spots so three teams could skate at the 2018 Olympics. We still beat a lot of really good teams and I was not anywhere near my top form. Part of me was disappointed with how it all unfolded. Ideally, we would have won again. But, under the circumstances I'm extremely proud and happy with how it ended.

"It wasn't until we returned to Montreal and I had imaging done that I learned I had a herniated disc that was pinching my nerve, making my muscles unresponsive. Then I freaked out because I didn't know if I could recover."

In February 2017 Meagan came home with Moo-tae, rescuing him from the Korean dog-meat industry. Even if you don't like dogs, you can't blame her for picking this pup. He was a cute addition to their menagerie that now included a cat and two dogs.

There were some lows for the duration of the 2016–2017 season that shook her badly and she declines to offer details. Sometimes, she too thought about retiring after Boston in April 2016, when spring was in the air, and they were atop the world in a shimmer of blue, hometown glory, and golden victory.

"Skating had been providing us with such a great life. Going to train wasn't a sacrifice. We were doing what we loved. We gave ourselves the freedom to perform in any show we wanted to while we were competing."

They recognized their good fortune. They had reached a point where skating was providing a good lifestyle and financial stability; they figured, "Why wouldn't we continue? We're halfway through the Olympic cycle. Why not finish it?"

Meagan remembers how well the season started in September. They landed the throw triple Axel in their short program at Skate Canada. They had a good long program, too, and left Skate Canada feeling confident.

Then the triple Axel's inconsistencies started to play with their confidence. After that everything just started to unravel. They went to NHK and fell on the triple Axel in the short program. Eric missed several elements in the long, which was uncharacteristic for him. Meagan says he might have missed a Lutz, on occasion, but he had never missed a triple Salchow or triple toe in their entire career.

This time, he did a double toe. They missed a lift at the end of the program. At the Grand Prix Final Meagan felt she skated horribly in both programs.

"Then, at Canadians, we felt like we had 'it' back. We removed the throw triple Axel and skated a clean short program. We scored eighty points, which was our highest score in Canada. We skated a good long program and set our first record for the number of Canadian pairs titles, at six.

"With the throw triple Axel out of the mix of elements, it felt like we had control again. But then we went to Four Continents and ran into trouble when Eric fell in the short program, which was again very unusual. It was such a weird season. We got it together at Skate Canada, and felt that we were still on the winning track. Then it all slipped through our fingers. Then we got it back for Canadians. Then it fell apart again at Four Continents."

Meagan says they didn't feel comfortable with their programs and they struggled to get on the same page for the Seal program. The long program was nice but it seemed to be lacking something special, something their Hometown Glory and Muse programs had. When they skated to "Hometown Glory" at the 2016 Worlds in Boston, they knew that they had the best long program in the field. That season, they knew when they entered every competition they had the best vehicle. If they delivered the goods, their program was the best.

"But in the 2016–2017 season, we went to every competition knowing we didn't have the best programs and that played with our confidence. We saw the great programs our competitors were putting out, and we knew we'd missed the ball."

After Four Continents Meagan sat down with Julie, Richard, Bruno and Eric and said, "I think we have to change our short program. We have a month until Worlds." She felt confident they could make an easy change, perhaps even return to the program from the year before.

Everyone else said, "No, we'll make Seal work."

Meagan agreed to give it more time, but her gut was telling her otherwise. Eric agreed with her but didn't feel they had enough time to switch, and he didn't feel safe taking that risk.

It's worth exploring what happens over a season. How is it that, after spending so much time developing a program, it doesn't work out? Skaters seem to practise so much, so hard. Meagan says when skaters start the season, they always expect the programs to grow along with them. They learn the choreography. They integrate the elements into the choreography. Once that's done, they start developing the nuances of the program. But that season their Seal short program never developed the way they envisioned it would.

"I personally loved the Seal short program. It's the way I want to skate. I loved it every time we skated. But it was the complete opposite to the way Eric skates and opposite to the way he feels music. We struggled to get on the same page with the program and have the same intensity. The feedback was always something like, 'You need more energy, more intensity, sharper movements.'

"Eric is a tall, graceful skater. All the sharp movements worked against what he does so well. We thought removing the throw triple Axel would give the program the space it needed to grow. It just didn't."

Sometimes programs do that. Meagan says for the Sochi 2014 season, they created the Alice in Wonderland program and skated it brilliantly. In practice. Meagan says that Richard would say it was his favourite of all their programs. But they never competed it well. When they were nervous the program never clicked. It was the same with their programs in 2016–2017. There were some great moments in practice but when Eric and Meagan were tense and nervous in competition, everything fizzled out of them.

They started to notice all this halfway through the season, just in time for the Four Continents and the Worlds. They started facing their main competition. Then they were too scared they would make a mistake. When Meagan and Eric skated like this, there was no freedom, no movement, no momentum. They would hold back and make mistakes because they were holding back. If they were cautious on the throws, Meagan would never land them. All their elements need momentum and freedom.

Over the years, Meagan endured a variety of little injuries in silence, declining to talk or complain about them. Before the 2017 Worlds, she developed what appeared to be another stress fracture in her foot that was aggravated by doing the triple toe loop in their jump combination. A MRI later revealed she had a piece of bone floating in her foot. Sometimes that little piece of bone would get stuck and when it did, it caused Meagan the pain. It could be the result of a lingering, old stress fracture. But at the time, they thought it was a new stress fracture.

She tried switching skates. They thought it might be a nerve issue. The pain came on slightly. Meagan couldn't practise triple toe jumps because her foot was hurting so badly. That was the only jump she could pick with her left foot on the take off. Every time she picked into the ice with her left foot to push off, pain would shoot through her leg.

But on the Salchow, she pushed off her blade and didn't pick into the ice. Picking into the ice seemed to cause that piece of bone to get stuck, possibly aggravating a nerve.

Most teams have one jump they do and they risk a second jump. Meagan and Eric had a handful to choose from so Meagan felt they were really lucky. One day they decided to change that jump to a triple Salchow; once they stopped practising the triple toe jump, the pain completely disappeared. They landed the Salchow and never went back to a triple toe.

When Meagan skated in ladies singles she once went to a competition with an air cast on her foot because she had a stress fracture. Unsurprisingly, she took off the cast and competed.

Regardless of all the little aches and pains, they flew into Worlds in Finland skating so well in training, and in their first practice in Finland. When they left the ice afterwards, Meagan was excited because she felt they could still contend for the world title. Their faith was restored after practice.

The next day, Eric couldn't do his Lutz jump, and worried they would be forced to withdraw. No one really knew what was wrong with Eric at the time.

"That's the thing, when you're involved in a team," Meagan reflects. "I was so ready to go. I was in the best physical and mental shape I could be in and Eric was in the lowest place he could be. I'm raring to go, to do whatever it takes. We were not on the same page."

Meagan thinks their programs were better than the results showed. The long program, other than the throw quad, was decent enough, so there was a wash of relief after a few days of stress and wondering what they were going to do. They competed. They finished seventh.

The experience at Worlds also proved the depth of Meagan's mental strength—even to herself. She hadn't tried a triple toe jump since December. Now it was the end of March, and in a high-pressure situation she made changes on the fly. She felt so proud of the mental strength that allowed her to keep up with everything going on around them.

After they finished, they realized their placing had helped qualify a third team for the 2018 Olympics. But the thought of qualifying the third team hadn't crossed Meagan's mind before they skated.

Meagan reflects that it's the same for any athlete in any sport. They have worked an entire season to reach the pinnacle. There's no giving up—they would find a way around any obstacle. That was her approach to the 2017 Worlds, as it would be for any elite athlete. Make adjustments and make it work to the best of your ability.

She never worried about her safety, even when Eric did. She says the worst of it for Eric seemed to be getting into rotation for the camel and sit spins and the jumps. They did some of their best throw twists in Finland.

In the side-by-side jumps, Meagan never paid attention to Eric. They were usually both so focused on themselves. At Worlds, this time she would look at him when they landed and acknowledge that, 'Okay, he's fine,' which she didn't normally do.

Meagan remembers Bruno telling Eric, "You're going out there in the long program and you'll go one element by one element. If you make it to the end, you make it to the end. And if you don't, you don't. But you go out there and you do each element one at a time until you cannot do another element." That approach took Meagan and Eric to the end of the program.

"I would have gone out there and skated by myself; over my dead body, was I going to withdraw from a competition. Even when I felt like I was dying of the flu at the Four Continents in Taipei, Taiwan in 2016, it still took me days to come to the conclusion that I couldn't skate. I couldn't even put one foot in front of the other to go to the bathroom. I still didn't want to withdraw. They had to force me to withdraw."

At the 2017 Worlds, it was obvious Eric was in pain; he was uncomfortable and uncertain. But Meagan was also fairly certain that Skate Canada and Bruno would ensure they would do whatever they could to try and compete. And that was exactly Bruno's approach.

"When Eric said, 'I don't know. What if after the side-by-side spin, I can't keep skating?' Bruno said, 'Deal with it then. But right now you're going on the ice and you're just doing a twist. Then you're just doing the jump. Then you're just doing each element until you literally can't do another element. And if you can't continue after the side-by-side spin, stop then. Don't stop now before we start.'"

After Worlds, Eric had a full month off. Then he and Meagan toured with Stars on Ice. Jumping and doing spins aggravated him the most but none of the elements in their show programs actually bothered him.

Meagan didn't like missing World Team Trophy because it was a fun competition and it would be their last time experiencing it. Naturally, they tried to find a way, but Skate Canada told the pair that they had to go at 100 per cent or not at all.

In the meantime, Meagan trained like she normally would. The Olympics were less than a year away and there wasn't a day to lose. As she was training, she began to entertain the thought of competing in ladies singles, as well as pairs. There was a third spot for Canadian ladies, behind Kaetlyn Osmond and Gabrielle Daleman, and Meagan seriously wondered about being the third woman. Throughout the entire Stars on Ice season she trained her jumps and learned the glorious, dizzying level four spins for singles skating.

Earlier in her career Meagan skated singles and pairs at the same time, but skating was so different back then. There were none of the transitions or choreography that are now features of the pairs that help connect the elements. Lifts were on two hands in the olden days.

And by the time the Olympics rolled around Meagan would be thirty-two years old, and even though she was serious about trying to see if it was possible, she thinks her body could not have handled the workload in a healthy manner.

After Stars on Ice, Eric and Meagan started the choreography for the Muse free skate right away. They were spending upwards of five hours on the ice a day, practising the choreography and reworking pair elements. On one particularly hard day, Meagan said, "There's no fricking way I'd have time to train a singles program. I could not do another two or three hours right now."

It was a smart move not to attempt both. Her foot was still a problem and she would need a triple-triple jump combination to even attempt to compete. She could do a double Axel triple toe in combination but one day in the spring of 2017, she landed the combination only to wake up the next day with pain back in her foot. She wouldn't have been able to consistently train the jumps that she needed to in order to be competitive in ladies singles.

"I'm certain I could have put up a good fight for that third spot for Canadian ladies. I can't guarantee I would have been the third Canadian woman, but I would have been in the mix. It was a fun dream. It would have made a great story. That's why I wanted to do it. How amazing would that have been? But how would that have impacted Eric's and my training for Korea?"

2017–2018: MUSING ON THE 'MUSE' AND OTHER CHANGES

Early in June 2017 Meagan and Eric approached Richard. He had been Eric's coach since 2008 and had coached Meagan since 2007. According to Meagan, Richard had believed in her when it seemed no one else would. "He took a big chance on me coming to skate with Craig. Craig was a national champion and an Olympian. I was nothing. And I was a bit out of shape. I owe my entire career to Richard for doing that."

Richard was such a key factor in their success, and in their career, but it had become evident in recent years that they weren't all on the same page anymore. Eric and Meagan say they were often left frustrated when working with Richard. There were many times throughout the past couple of years where they felt they needed "more" from their coach.

Eric hesitated. There had been some communication issues in the skating lessons with Richard, but Eric felt that since he was a little bit easier going, he could go with the flow. He liked Richard's energy. There were times they clashed and wouldn't agree with Richard's decisions. But Eric usually shrugged it off.

Their working relationship was starting to feel stale, and with everything that had happened at Worlds and the breakdown in communication, the decision became clearer for Eric.

"I think it was partly that we're older and as a senior team, each year is about recreating yourself and then coming up with something new and original."

They wondered how to tell Richard the change was coming. For weeks, they had thought of other ways to keep him with them. They had dreaded and put off the meeting. "There was no good way to do it, and it was going to be really difficult to do it. And it was. We told him we wanted a meeting with him. Perhaps he had an inkling. He's always so upbeat. He has an infectious energy. He was happy to see us," Eric recalls.

"We sat down and we started talking about the future right away. Then we had to solemnly say we won't be continuing with him, and that we would be making changes to our training."

Despite his obvious hurt, Richard was gracious and said that he hoped he would be at the Olympics to see them win a medal.

Then it was back to work. They drove in their separate cars to Sainte-Julie and went to work on their new choreography, even though Julie Marcotte hadn't wanted them to come to the rink that morning. "She didn't want us showing up being sour and bringing a bad energy with us when we were trying to create these beautiful programs for the Olympics," Meagan says. "But it was almost a relief. It really felt like a fresh start. We talked to Julie when we got to the rink. She asked us how it went. We went over it with her."

Although they were senior athletes, having a coach is like having reassurance. When Meagan was on the ice for the six-minute warm up, she would never go to the boards to visit the coaches but she would always look for a head nod or a little arm movement correction from Bruno.

"Also, at this point in our careers, we weren't going to do something drastic like move to Russia or China to train. We weren't going to uproot our lives for eight months," she says.

Obviously Bruno is Meagan's husband but, as she says, he was also their coach. She did not make the decision alone. "Bruno taught us the throw quad and the throw triple Axel. Eric trusts Bruno's coaching style and believes that when he's having trouble with anything to do with skating technique, it's Bruno who can fix it."

Eric says that people could think that the pair only stayed with Bruno and Julie because they're family but it wasn't a decision that was solely Meagan's. "It was a decision made by a working relationship. It had nothing to do with any personal relationship. It comes down to how we feel and what we needed in our final season of competition," Meagan adds.

With only eight months to go to the Olympics and their final competition, the coaching change made headlines. Skate Canada reported, "Meagan Duhamel and Eric Radford update coaching team"; The *Toronto Star* announced, "Meagan Duhamel, Eric Radford oust coach eight months of Olympics," and from the CBC, "Figure Skaters Duhamel, Radford turf coach in bold shakeup." In some circles it was called a firing, although Meagan and Eric said that was not the word they used. The word that mattered to them was "comfort".

Over the fall of 2017 and into 2018, I had numerous conversations with Meagan and Eric (usually separately, when busy schedules made it necessary) about their coaching change and what happened at the 2017 Worlds. Sometimes our conversations went quite late, until after 8 p.m. (this qualifies as late for athletes who need their sleep).

On this particular night, via Skype from his couch at home in Montreal, Eric has finished reflecting on leaving Richard and how that was one of his hardest decisions in skating. Leaving Rachel and moving to Montreal when he was twenty-two was another one.

Eric pauses and then proceeds to give a surprising picture of what rock bottom actually looked like for an elite athlete heading into his final competitive season.

He and Meagan were starting to feel more connected again and it was like the early days of their partnership. But the summer of 2017 was difficult. He didn't want to sugarcoat the truth of his story. "It hasn't always been, 'Yay! We won a competition.' It's been really difficult sometimes."

Meagan and Eric were now training exclusively in Sainte-Julie. As Eric worked his back into shape, he wore a brace and had started seeing an osteopathic doctor every day. He was managing the physical side.

"The emotional pain was still there. We had fallen from grace, so to speak. We were at the bottom of a mountain, looking up at the pinnacle, where we used to be, and I wasn't entirely confident I would be able to get back to the top again. That feeling weighed on me and I was also trying not to think about the fact that it was an Olympic season, and most likely our last-ever competitive season.

"As we began piecing the programs together I was feeling more stress than usual that things needed to be better. I wanted to make sure everything was at a high level and I really had to believe in everything we were doing."

In addition to managing the recovery of his back, he was trying to get his jumps back. His triple Lutz was so far gone after the injury that it took most of the summer to get it back to where he could land it every day. He needed new skates, but when he got them, they didn't feel right. Then he and Meagan skated poorly because he didn't feel comfortable.

He had moved into a new apartment that spring, which demanded more energy after he had been skating all day. He would come home, paint the apartment, and deal with the complete renovation of the bathroom. His home was a mess.

"There was such a culmination of things happening. Almost every aspect of my life was a struggle and difficult. Then I just snapped. I ended up having a nervous breakdown.

"In June, it started subtly enough one day while I was having a massage. I was feeling anxious to begin with and began thinking about all that I had going on. I was feeling guilty that I hadn't answered all my emails. I was overwhelmed by training. I had constant pain in my back.

"I had trouble sleeping that night, and when I woke up the next day I had a full blown panic attack. It felt like the world was ending and I couldn't think of anything that would make me feel better. I'm usually in control of my emotions and to have them go haywire like that left me feeling out of control and vulnerable."

He called his sports psychologist immediately and was lucky to get him right away. The psychologist started talking Eric down, telling him, "This is what is happening to you. You're not dying." It took about ten minutes.

It was the beginning of almost two months of working to get back to where Eric felt normal, and of dealing with constant anxiety for the first time in his career.

It's tricky to interrupt and ask him questions that arose, but there is a moment to slip in a query about what he did about it. He made himself reach out to family and friends. Bruno and Meagan were incredibly supportive. Meagan gave him books and other resources on mindfulness and meditation.

Eric spoke with his sports psychologist every day. He would call his doctor friends every day. When he wasn't on the ice he was on his phone talking and talking and slowly healing mentally. It seemed to take so long for the anxiety to subside.

It became difficult to wake up in the morning with the feeling that there was no point to anything. Yet he couldn't sit still. His mind was racing all the time. Remarkably, and likely for the first time in his life, playing the piano didn't spark any happiness. Thinking about friends or family didn't spark anything either. It was like dead silence inside, he says.

"I think it was a perfect storm of my physical, emotional and mental state and everything being pushed to the breaking point, and then everything crumbled. I remember describing it as feeling that I was being crushed by the weight of my own life.

"The thing is, I'm a critical thinker and I'm well aware of everything I had to appreciate in my life. There was this separation between mind and heart. I couldn't change how I felt. That was very scary and frustrating for me because I'm usually in tune with myself and in control of my emotions. When something bad does happen I'm very good at understanding it and letting it go. This was a case where I was completely out of control and it was terrifying."

Valerie and Rick came to stay for about ten days and helped out at home. Eric skated every day but struggled with his jumps. The lifts and twists were still there but every day felt like a battle. For about two long weeks he was mired in negative feelings. He only felt normal when he was looking at his phone, trying to keep his mind busy so he couldn't think about himself, his surroundings, or what he was feeling. His doctor had prescribed anti-anxiety medication, which he usually took at night so he could sleep.

"About a month or so later, I was skating around the rink, just warming up my jumps and all of a sudden, it was like a switch turning on. I felt a little lift and my mood changed. The feeling lasted only a few minutes but it was the first time I'd felt any relief from the constant anxiety. 'There we go,' I thought. 'That's all I needed to know. I'm starting to get better.'

"From there it got lighter and lighter until eventually it was gone, just before our summer provincials."

At the end of August they went to Florida to train with John Kerr and John Zimmerman. Eric was starting to feel better but was anxious on the plane about leaving home and how he would cope. Pictures on Facebook and Instagram showed Meagan and Eric enjoying Florida, driving in a convertible, so it's a surprise to know that he was also trying to move up from rock bottom. He has trained himself to smile when he doesn't always feel like it, he says.

Eric felt almost normal again while skating in Florida; he was keeping his body and mind busy. As soon as they stopped and he took off his skates, the waves of anxiety would wash over him again. It was always there.

He realized, he says from the other side of the anxiety late in 2017, that leaving the rink at Saint-Leonard meant they were also leaving all the skaters they used to socialize with at the rink.

For a time in Sainte-Julie, only Meagan and Eric, a couple of junior teams, and the North Korean pair Bruno was coaching, were on the ice. Eric would come to the rink, not talk to anybody, and just skate. It felt very militaristic. The social aspect had changed.

"Skating felt like a job," Eric remembers. "It's almost like I was having a midlife crisis where everything fell apart and I was left rethinking how I felt about everything."

After Eric finishes relating all this via Skype, there is a long pause to reflect. Then we wander through a brief discussion of research about the roles severe pain and a loss of control—which Eric experienced with his back—play in causing traumatic stress and anxiety. He thinks there may be something to that. I ask why he wants to share this aspect of their story. It all feels private, more personal than even one's orientation. Does he really want to share this?

"The most inspiring stories come from people who you perceive to be invincible. Not that anyone perceives me like that but in general, you see someone who is invincible, then you realize they are human and they are just as sensitive and vulnerable as you are. But they persevere and they push through and it can teach you that everything is going to be okay. The moment will pass and things will get better.

"For me, it was matter of time, support from my friends and family, and of slowly getting stronger again. The whole process of putting the short together with John and Julie made me feel like our skating was taking a giant step forward in the direction I've always wanted it to. That sense of accomplishment got the ball rolling. We were skating with a greater sense of purpose and freedom."

There would be a lot of praise for their new short program, choreographed to U2's "With Or Without You," performed by April Meservy. The elements flowed effortlessly and it was always a surprise when the program ended. It was one that could have gone on, such was the way it moved across the ice. Every time they skated the program, even during run-throughs in practice, Eric and Meagan felt that flow. The elements came close together and there wasn't much time to do a lot of other movements, yet there was purpose even in the short little transitions between the required elements. There was a feeling in each moment.

For Eric, sometimes the robotic aspect of needing to skate cleanly would overtake the artistic challenges they had imbedded in the program. They always had to find that balance. But this new, Olympic short program flowed and connected perfectly, better than any program they had ever done, Eric reflects.

John Kerr had a unique energy and the way he built the program with Meagan, Julie and Eric seemed to unify the team. They were back on the same page again. Julie had a target in mind when she first discovered April Meservy's version of "With or Without You."

From the very beginning of skating that program, Eric had an instant, tangible and clear focus and connection with Meagan. That short program ended up being his favourite of all their pieces over the eight years. It was the vehicle and the catalyst for putting them back together on the same page after everything they had endured the season before.

As they started to piece it together, to do the run-throughs and the elements, it was like a little slow snowball effect where Eric could start to see that they could be successful again.

"Now that I'm on the other side of everything it's easy to say of course everything was going to work out. Hindsight is always 20-20, but in that moment, when you don't know what the future holds and you don't know what is going to happen, it just feels like the end of the world.

"You feel lost. When the question, 'Why am I doing this?' isn't clear, that causes me the most problems. For Meagan the why is always very, very clear. She's always been extremely motivated. She has never had a day where she hasn't felt motivated, because the reason she's in the rink is always very clear, even in those hard moments."

Eric's injury, combined with the disconnect between the partners, made them wonder how they would ever get back to where they had been as skaters. The short program was simply that huge step toward the podium.

The Muse program, on the other hand, was trying to tell them something. They had won their first World Championships and skated undefeated that season with that program. But when it came to constructing the programs for the Olympics, they wanted to change Muse so that it didn't look the same and in doing so, they ruined it, Meagan says.

"The main lesson that we learned from the Muse program was that you don't change something that works. We tried to reconstruct it. We tried to put the throw quad during the slow part of the music, just to do something different. We don't get a bonus for doing elements in the second half of the pairs program. We ordered the elements differently than we had been doing and of course, we thought we'd make it work."

It was harder than they thought. Even though they were training spectacular short programs every day, their long program remained "crappy" in training throughout August and September, says Meagan.

They kept thinking everything would come together. They had redone the choreography, but now that it was so much more complex it never naturally flowed. It looked and felt like work, which made it harder to execute all the elements smoothly. In practice the program looked clunky—even to a less than experienced figure skating eye. The Muse music was fast and there was no chance within the body of the program to reset if they ever made a mistake. They learned this the hard way when they performed it at the Autumn Classic International in September. There were three hard falls, including two in a row early in the program.

Meagan Duhamel and Eric Radford with Laura E. Young

"After our skate, we were sitting in the kiss and cry waiting for our scores and I said, 'We have to go back to our long program, to Adele. Muse wasn't the right program. We made the wrong choice.'

"Everyone told me I was getting carried away in the heat and emotion of the moment. They comforted me saying we'd reset Muse and it would all work out. I said, 'Okay, I have voiced my opinion,' and I let it be," Meagan remembers.

They reset Muse back to the original program that had won the 2015 Worlds. The run-throughs became clean every day. They won Skate Canada and scored 148 points in the free skate. At Skate America they finished third but still scored over 140 points for the free skate, which was more than they had scored in the 2016–2017 season.

They finished third at the Grand Prix Final even though they didn't skate either program perfectly. But they skated well enough to enjoy a mental boost from their performances, and they sent a message. They had defeated both Russian teams to come from fifth into third. They began to feel that perhaps they really would end up on the Olympic podium in the individual pairs event. Meagan thinks it was an important moment for them and for the skating community.

The Muse program still wasn't clicking the way their new short program was, though. It was obvious that they felt connected to the emotion of the "With or Without You" short program. They were competing well, but they didn't have the emotional, uplifting experience that they wanted to feel, especially at the Olympics, skating to Muse.

They had chosen two different sets of music and created two different programs to reflect diversity as skaters. But Meagan and Eric were at the point where they wanted to be comfortable and emotionally invested in both programs.

After the Grand Prix Final they went to China to perform in some shows with no intention of switching programs. They thought about trying to calm down the timing on the throw quad because they had been getting a little carried away in the Grand Prix competitions. Meagan took a particularly hard fall to her chest in the free skate of the Grand Prix Final, which she would later say hurt as bad as it looked on TV. She was bruised the day after.

At a dress rehearsal in China, they were scheduled to skate right after Ekaterina Gordeeva, the 1988 and 1994 Olympic pairs champion. As they waited behind the curtain on a small patch of ice, Gordeeva practised her number. She just happened to be doing a show program to Adele's "Hometown Glory."

"When I heard it from behind the curtain, everything just soothed inside my soul. That was it for me. I wanted to feel this way at the Olympics. I knew what we had to do. We needed to skate to that piece of music," Meagan says.

After the rehearsal Meagan told Eric what she was thinking. He'd had the exact same thought. They watched their 2016 World Championships program on YouTube and started piecing the program back together that very day. Everything came back. Everything flowed.

Canadians was in less than three weeks but for some reason they didn't panic. It all just felt right.

They texted Bruno and Julie: "Look guys, we're going back to Adele. It's the right thing. We'll see you next week at the rink." Bruno and Julie responded, "If you feel like it's right, we support that decision."

Meagan remembers thinking at one point, "Ekaterina will probably never know the effect that this moment had on our careers." There were fifteen skaters in the show. Meagan and Eric only followed her that one time, to "Hometown Glory." A lot of fate goes into these things, Meagan says.

Back in Montreal, Eric and Meagan were temporarily without a choreographer as Julie had gone to Japan for an event. They were left to relearn the program and its nuances themselves. There were a few things that had changed: different jumps, different death spirals.

Julie came back from Japan in late December, and Meagan and Eric were like children at Christmas: "Look at what we did!" Julie never told them whether she questioned their decision, but Meagan and Eric remember how Julie went with the flow because her skaters had so naturally gone with the flow. Julie ironed out some issues with timing and patterns, added some nuances and arm and head movements, Meagan says.

"It wasn't ideal but we didn't panic. We were so calm about it which shocked me. We reset the program and we were running it full within a week. We'd never done that before, but we had no choice. Canadians were coming and we just did it."

All along Eric and Megan had planned to retrieve one of their best programs for the Olympics. The first Muse had won them a world title and had been the long program for the undefeated season. Their ho-hum skate in Sochi, their drive to learn a throw quadruple Salchow and a sense of newfound freedom had fuelled the Muse program's fire.

In 2017–2018, they weren't there anymore. They wanted to feel comfortable on the ice, in their skating. There were only three weeks to Canadians. But as Eric says, their moves to "Hometown Glory" came back easily, naturally, from the first run-through.

"Right away I felt like we had a better grasp of the program. There was more depth for me to work with. It's hard to put it into words. It's funny. When I go back and compare the Boston version with this season, I feel like we took a big step forward. I feel like we had more integrity in the performance from the very beginning. We were able to perform it with more purpose.

"I don't know if it's like riding a bike—once you've mastered it, you can always pick it up again. We had wanted to be comfortable in our last season. Returning to "Hometown Glory" after trying to make Muse work lent itself to that simpler feel."

Then it was off to Vancouver for their final Canadians. While not exactly taking it for granted, Meagan and Eric knew it was likely they would win their seventh Canadian title. But, Eric was in an odd mindset ahead of their final championships—while he felt confident in their skating, he was concerned for the other teams. There was a peculiar sense of unease at not knowing what was going to happen with the other skaters. Eric knew the competition would be intense for Kirsten Moore-Towers and Mike Marinaro, who were their training partners, and for Dylan Moscovitch, who remained Eric's best friend, and his partner Liubov Ilyushechkina. Feeling so invested in their situation was something new for Eric.

"Knowing it was our last Canadians, I enjoyed the greatest feeling of being home and the warm energy from the audience. In the long program we were backstage waiting to skate when I saw Dylan walk by. He looked completely defeated. They wound up fourth and off the Olympic team. The other teams skated very well. I remember skating around waiting for Julie and Charlie's marks before our program and thinking of my best friend and everything that had happened to him and Liubov."

Feeling too much already, Eric managed to turn off his emotions. Their free skate went well, except for a fall on the throw quad, and they easily claimed their seventh Canadian title, making history. The celebration was a little muted for Eric, though. He was devastated for Dylan. Eric found Dylan in the change room and gave him a big hug.

Afterwards Eric met with his parents and friends. It seemed to Eric that everyone was thinking he was crying tears of joy, but he was actually upset about his best friend not making it to the Olympics. Valerie Radford knew, however, and she was upset, too. She said, "It's Dylan, isn't it?"

Eric says Canadians were strangely emotional in a way he hadn't experienced before. "I have the fondest, best memories from Canadians, that I'll remember forever. It's like a piece of art that is now complete. I'm totally satisfied with how this piece of art looks. I don't need to add anything else to it. I have a deep sense of completion, not just with Canadians, but with my whole competitive career."

2018 OLYMPICS: WRITING THE STORYBOOK ENDING

What drives athletes? To understand what motivates elite athletes you would choose from a variety of options: they compete for themselves, for their country, always for their ultimate personal best performance. In Meagan's case, there was a sprinkling of lingering bitterness from Sochi, not just about the fact that she missed a triple Salchow jump in combination, but also the outcome of the team event.

Over that final season, team veterans Meagan, Eric, Scott Moir, Tessa Virtue, and Patrick Chan would talk more about the team event in Korea. There was a lot of strategizing about whether the skaters would perform two skates, or just one program and then rest for their respective individual events.

One day, Scott met Eric and Meagan at the gym and over the course of the conversation told them that he didn't want Eric and Meagan to feel pressured to compete too much and sacrifice their individual event for the team. Of course, in a form of laying down a friendly intra-team gauntlet, Meagan and Eric told him that they were planning to do all four skates and that they expected him and Tessa to do the same. Everybody was on the same page, understanding that the rarest of medals was on the line, an Olympic gold medal. It was a gold medal that Canada well knew was there for the taking because Canada had strength and depth across all four skating disciplines. No one would turn the golden opportunity down.

Not surprisingly—in fact, it would have been a shock if they had skated only once—Eric and Meagan relished doing everything: four skates and all that entailed in terms of practice and preparation. They were going to the Olympics in the best shape of their lives, mentally and physically, and, as Meagan says, they were never going to skate at the Olympics again so why wouldn't they skate as much as they could?

Besides, they had always wanted to do four events. Canada was going for the gold; ultimately it would be Canada's first gold medal won at the PyeongChang Games. But in order for Canada to earn the maximum amount of points, Meagan and Eric would have to skate both the short and long programs.

Eric felt they were part of perhaps the best all-around team Canada had ever fielded in skating, and certainly the most rounded team competing in the team event in Korea. Eric recalls how contagious Scott's energy was at the Montreal gym where they all worked out.

"Scott was saying, 'We're going for this. We're going for gold in the team event, enjoy the moment and then skate our individual events.'"

The individual athletes were acting like a team. They would talk to one another about their respective schedules and who was rooming with whom. They all planned how they would manage their energy at the games. The excitement was building. For Eric, it was such a nice feeling to approach this huge moment in their careers, to feel part of a team, rather than just Meagan and Eric.

Meagan and Eric changed nothing as they prepared for the games. They knew their schedules so there would be no surprises in Korea. They were skating so well leading into the Olympics and there was a growing feeling they could have a great skate. At any competition where they had skated well, they had been well-prepared at home. There was a sense, an intuition that they would have a great Olympics, Meagan remembers. They just had to get through that team event first, which isn't the norm for figure skaters.

On their last training day back home in Montreal, they had kept things quiet and low key. Bruno would later tell Meagan the coaches had thought about doing a big send off. They were wondering if they should celebrate Meagan and Eric? But in the end the coaches had decided that Meagan and Eric needed a stable routine. "I didn't want to throw you off, so we kept the training day normal," Bruno said.

Leaving for the games, Meagan spied a *People* magazine in the airport store. The magazine featured Olympic success stories, including those of figure skaters. She knew most of the stories but bought it anyway. On the plane she began reading about the 2010 Olympic men's champion, American Evan Lysacek.

In Vancouver Evan had taken a piece of paper and written 'mind your own business.' He made that his focus and mantra for the entire Olympics. Meagan was then inspired to write Eric a letter that she gave to him in Korea, which basically said the same thing: while they were in PyeongChang, they would mind their business. They built themselves an Olympic bubble of their own, within the Olympic bubble.

They carefully managed their energy while they were in Korea. It took focus and concentration to not let it all slip away into the Olympic vortex. If they wanted to relax, to keep it quiet, they did. At one point in the team event, Meagan appeared so relaxed that she was eating cookies while cheering on her teammates. If Eric sensed too much energy, he went to his room.

Meagan says they didn't lose that focus until they were finished competing. "It was very easy to remind ourselves that if you felt your attention going towards something else, it was

'Nope, I'm just going to mind my own business.' It kept our energy and our world so small and compact."

In the moments leading up to their final long program, for instance, the Germans scored a world-record for a free skate. Meagan and Eric were happy for their friends and rivals, but told themselves, "Nope, I'm minding my own business. We can skate great as well."

"Skating in the team event and then the individual event is a big deal for us. Physically it was less than most skaters do every week. It was more the emotional and mental ability—swimmers and track and field athletes will race, perhaps win a medal and do it all over again. This is what they know.

"This was the furthest from what we knew as skaters. We do programs every day but being on the biggest stage in the world, and standing on the Olympic podium is not the same as practising at home."

In PyeongChang, Meagan and Eric were scheduled for two training sessions a day but usually only skated one thirty-minute practice. They would calmly do everything that needed to be done in that thirty minutes. They usually didn't need another practice, so they would just rest. At one practice, Eric couldn't land a triple Lutz jump but that was their only hitch. Their elements were all firing—the triple twist, the triple Lutzes, the throw quad. They felt confident, she remembers.

"I don't know if the environment plays into that. The arena was pretty empty. The rink in Sochi was rowdy, riled up and it seemed that they only liked the Russians. The energy was so different at these games. Maybe that's what it feels like when you go to your second Olympics. Everything felt less of a big deal this time."

Canada won the team gold in PyeongChang. Eric says they had already decided they would live it up and enjoy their golden moment. "I allowed myself to really take it all in, to laugh and get excited, and because I knew I had two days after that to prepare for the individual event.

"There was a lot of energy. That was a crazy time. As soon as we were back on the bus heading down to the Athletes' Village, I would just listen to music and I kept myself very calm. It was just being aware of your energy and not being caught up in moments and with people.

"When that was over, it was time to get back to work. But there was so much energy around that moment. We had won Canada's first gold medal of the games. I was getting ready for bed and went onto my social media, which had just exploded. You can feel it just lying in bed—you can feel the energy of what you've just accomplished coming back to you."

Meagan and Eric headed into the individual pairs event with a shot at the bronze, though in some circles they were predicted to finish fifth, at best fourth. The evening was shaping up to be among the best, tightest pairs competitions in many an Olympics. There was no room for error. Aljona Savchenko and Bruno Massot of Germany found themselves a fortunate fourth after making one glaring mistake on their side-by-side jumps in the short program.

In a slight break from their Olympic routine, Meagan and Eric switched their one-a-day practice the day before the short program in their individual event. The morning practice went perfectly. Eric thought they didn't need to practise again. But since they had already scheduled a second practice, they decided to stick to the plan. "Something felt different when I stepped on the ice. My energy was off, but I thought I could just focus and get through it," he recalls.

Then his ability to complete a triple Lutz seemed to vanish. "I popped or failed to launch my first triple Lutz, which was no big deal, but then on the second one, I just about killed myself, body slamming into the ice. Bruno reminded me of my key words to focus on when I did the jump.

"The next jump, body slam, again and again. I must have tried twenty-five triple Lutzes and I didn't land a single one."

Eric thinks Bruno was at a loss for words, too. "I was trying to stay calm and not freak out and even though I was a shaken, there was a quiet little voice telling me I would be fine the next day," Eric says. "And that little voice, that ball of yes, was right. The next morning at practice I landed the first one I tried."

To open the individual event on February 14, Meagan and Eric skated a calculated, solid short program and went into the Olympic long program in third place, just ahead of Aljona and Bruno. Sui Wenjing and Han Cong of China led and Evgenia Tarasova and Vladimir Morozov, the Olympic Athletes from Russia (OAR) were second.

Bruno draws on a hockey analogy, comparing that figure skating final to a game 7 in overtime. One mistake would have sent them spiralling out of the picture.

Meagan says they set their minds to focusing on winning a bronze medal. She laughs that maybe she should have imagined winning the gold medal. "Maybe we would have, but, no, I was also realistic. We kind of knew what the judges would score us. I felt so sure we would have great skates but I wasn't certain of what the judges would do with those great skates.

"But the feeling was building within me that the skates would happen, I knew it. That's why we were able to stay so calm. There was no panic, there were no nerves, it was like we were just riding a wave."

On the day of the long program, Meagan and Eric practised well and then went back to their rooms, just as they always did between the events. There wasn't much turnaround time but they were determined to stick to their routine.

As they drove back to their rooms they looked at each other and told each other they were going to do it. There was a calm, quiet confidence between the skaters, as there had been before all of their career successes—from Boston in 2016 to their undefeated 2014–2015 season and all the battles against stiff competition to win Canadian titles, Meagan says.

"You always wish you could push a button and get yourself there but it's not that easy. The steps to get to that point are so difficult. Usually at competitions I'm anxious, I'm irritable. I just didn't feel that in Korea. I was sleeping well. I was relaxed. Sometimes at competitions I visualize falling on a spin, forgetting my program, anything bad happening, but I was only visualizing great performances while I was in Korea.

"When we were on the podium to get the gold medal in the team event, I was thinking, 'In a few days I'm going to come back here and I'm going to win that bronze medal.' I knew it. I could say it out loud with certainty."

It seemed their destiny was to skate right after other great performances. At the 2012 Canadians they had to beat Dylan and Kirsten who had just set a Canadian record and scored higher than Meagan and Eric ever had. At the Grand Prix Final in 2014 a Russian team skated brilliantly ahead of the Canadians and scored higher than they ever had. Then Meagan and Eric went out and beat that score.

On that February night, Aljona and Bruno were also sentimental favourites for the gold. Aljona was at her fifth Olympics and had won two Olympic bronze medals with her previous partner, Robin Szolkowy, who had retired and was coaching their OAR rivals, Evgenia and Vladimir.

Aljona and Bruno had struggled with their short program throughout the Olympics, so when she and Bruno finally had their Olympic moment Meagan and Eric could only rejoice. Meagan felt happy for her competitors. There was comfort in the familiarity of knowing she and Eric were at the Olympics in their last event, skating after somebody else's great performance. It was the story of their lives, Meagan says.

"There have been times when Eric and I are waiting on the ice to be announced and we'd hear the score of the previous team. Then I start doing the math in my head as I figure out what I need to score to beat them.

"At the Olympics this time, all their scores did was motivate me to have a great moment just like they did. The energy was so high you just wanted to take it and ride with it. When I heard their score, it went in one ear and out the other. I didn't care at all. I was already not over-thinking our performance."

But sometimes there's no way to know why things happen as they do. When the time came for their signature side-by-side triple Lutz, Meagan completely missed her toe pick on the takeoff. It actually looked like the toe of her boot was on the ice, not her blade. She didn't get to transfer into the jump rotation at all. She managed to land the jump, but at home, she would have missed it completely, she says.

The near miss on Olympic ice came as a wake-up call. Usually the triple twist takes care of that with a bobble on the catch but in the Olympic long program, their twist was excellent. The Lutz proved to be the reality check. Meagan's near miss shook her up because she never should have landed it. It was all willpower, she says.

Meagan Duhamel and Eric Radford with Laura E. Young

From that point there were only about ten seconds before the throw quadruple Salchow. They flowed into the element maintaining the speed. Eric set the pattern into its cozy little pocket of perfection and Meagan went straight through to her jump.

They had worked hard on this entrance to the throw. The more it worked the more confident they became and the easier the element became to execute if they were nervous. The Olympic ice surface is larger than the ice they trained on at home. That size difference led to problems over the years with the throw quad in competition. On bigger ice the pattern changed and they couldn't manage the throw. Meagan says they had rarely landed the quad on Olympic-size ice in competition.

"This time we were so aware of not trying to fill the ice or stay as close to the boards as we do at home. Just forget about it. We were so hyper-aware of these things."

In PyeongChang, nailing the throw quad didn't mean they could relax. Five seconds later came the three-jump combination that Meagan had fallen on in Sochi, tumbling on the first element, the side-by-side triple Salchow. This miss remained her big hurdle mentally. She couldn't wait to return to the Olympics and land that damn triple Salchow, she says. The miss had caused her so-called failure in her long program in Sochi, and had eaten away at Meagan for years. She refused to let that happen again. The combination was valuable, worth eight points alone. After that, the second throw, the throw triple Lutz, was Meagan's last big element to land. Then Eric does all the lifting and spinning for the two.

At that point, Meagan made a mental check. "That's when I was thinking, 'Okay just stay focused now until the end.' You want to get carried away emotionally because you're having this great program, but you also don't want to make a careless mistake.

"So after that we were teetering between letting it all go and releasing everything and, 'No, there's this and this to do. We need to get all our levels. We need to hold our spins long enough, we need to sit low enough, we need to let go of the arm quick enough in the lifts.' A lot of tiny details in those elements are easier to do than a throw quad, but they're still important.

"I wouldn't say I was really nervous about anything in the program, but going into our final move, the back outside death spiral, I was thinking, 'Okay don't ruin this moment right now.' That would have never entered my mind on an easier death spiral.

"As we went down in the death spiral I was very focused. We had to make sure our circle was big enough, our speed was good enough, our hand grip was correct. A lot of little things are in that element. It appears so nice and easy, but it's actually nerve-wracking. And when we reset the program, there was nowhere else to put it, except the end. Every day we would train the long program in practice and then go back out and do another death spiral. Just to be sure.

"Usually after the last throw my focus is elation, 'Oh, my God! We did it. Now we just have to get to the end. The difficult stuff is over.' But for me, the last element, the back outside death spiral, is so hard. Our program had the flow and emotion but I was still very focused on that back outside at the end. Whereas in Boston in 2016, going with an easier death spiral at the end, I could care less, I was already celebrating. I could do that death spiral with no effort."

As glorious as the quintessential pairs element is, the death spiral is also extremely tricky. At any moment the female partner could lose the edge. The balance point is different in this type of spiral, so the skaters have to work throughout the whole thing. Their legs are burning. The female partner needs to get low enough to hold the edge. At any moment she could slip outside the circle she's tracing. The male partner is trying to sit low enough, while looking wonderful, to get all the marks available. When fatigue has set in, it's very difficult for Eric to sit that low.

For Eric, the triple Salchow, double toe, double toe jump combination after the throw quad was one of the best they had ever done. But he was feeling that way throughout the entire long program final.

"I felt so in the moment and strong. Compared to the team event, in the final, I felt like I had a greater capacity to really perform and enjoy the moment. I think we played it a little bit safer in the team long program. The throw quad worked so well in the month leading up to the Olympics that it had become automatic. Just as I threw Meagan I had a little moment of, 'Yes!' It was right on the exact pattern it needed to be.

"In the final, I put Meagan down out of the second lift, and as we skated around the corner into the throw, I looked up towards the ceiling and just had a release. We had moments like that throughout that long program.

"I made sure I was smiling when we were in that final lift, and I'm in the spreadeagle position, holding Meagan up. If people were going to get a photo of this, I wanted them to see that I was smiling instead of really working. That was how comfortable I was—I could have thoughts like that."

There was a lot of collapsing on the ice that night. Aljona and Bruno had dropped to the ice at the end of their mesmerizing performance. Meagan, too, dropped to her knees.

"I always imagine what I'm going to do at the end of a performance. I think I'm going to stand there and be so excited. I'm going to jump on Eric.

"The long program music stopped and I definitely hit an emotional wall, not a physical one. There was relief. It worked—we did it. There was a little bit of disbelief where I was like, 'How did we do that throw quad and how did I miss the Lutz?' I never end up reacting the way I think I will at the end of a great performance. In that moment it's so organic. I don't know what my body was doing but that's what happened.

"After we finished, I jumped into Bruno's arms. The first thing he said to me was, 'You are the most mentally tough skater I've ever seen. You should have never landed that triple Lutz. How did you do that?'"

After they had thanked everyone at home in Sainte-Julie and across Canada, Meagan told Bruno and co-coach Ian Connolly that if they were fourth, it would be the greatest in history. Bruno wondered to himself if it had been enough. All week he'd had a sense that

Meagan Duhamel and Eric Radford with Laura E. Young

they were being underscored on the second or grade of execution mark. He thought they would have to emphasize their technical prowess and then hope.

For Meagan, fourth would have dampened the moment, but what she meant was they had done their job. Now they would have to wait for the bronze medal, the cherry on top of the sundae of their Olympic moment. Meagan says they would be proud of that skate for the rest of their lives.

"If we were rewarded fourth place for that, then it was out of our control. It was something we hoped we could be awarded for—we did our job. I was still pretty certain that we were going to get the bronze medal at that point. Our chance at a medal came from beating the Russians. They had to skate perfectly to score what they needed to because their scoring potential was just not as high as ours.

"We've had the wrong programs in the past. We tried to be dramatic with the Alice in Wonderland program, but no matter how well-trained and confident we were, we could never perform that program well in competition. We just didn't flow with it. We didn't feel it. I know what it's like to have the wrong program. I knew that was the case for the Russian team with their free skate this year, so it was highly unlikely they would skate well under all the pressure and with the wrong program, through my own experience.

"After the short program the Russians were five points ahead of us, but I was okay with that. We made up more than that to pass them at the Grand Prix Final in December, so I had no doubt it was possible to do it again."

That night commentators and social media lit up with the history-making of Meagan and Eric's Olympic skate and final competitive performance. Regardless of where they would place, they were now the first pair to have landed the throw quadruple Salchow cleanly in the Olympics. It was yet another bonus for Eric who was enjoying his status as the first openly gay athlete to win a gold medal at the Winter Games. Then they had to wait to see if there was also a bronze in his future.

They had scored 153.33, just shy of their personal best, and matching their score from Boston 2016. Now they had to wait. Eric peeled off his skates, rolled up his pants to his knees and leaned back on the couches in the "purple room," where a German team official was filming reactions. The skaters tried to relax on the stuffed chaises to await the marks of the proceeding skaters. No one was allowed to leave unless they were bumped out by a pair that had finished with a higher score.

That time in the purple room would ultimately become one of Eric's favourite Olympic moments. They could see the technical score counter in real time for the other teams. The energy between the Germans and the Chinese was so intense. Aljona and Bruno were almost distraught with happiness and Sui and Han were heartbroken. Meagan and Eric were excited. Eric felt like they were these little kids.

"To have one of our best scores in the most important moment at the most important event is just the best feeling. Of course, we always want to aim higher and if we'd done a perfect Lutz then maybe our score would have been 155. If. Who knows? Maybe we could have broken our record with the perfect, perfect skate. But I think that it was pretty much as good as we could have hoped for."

Unfortunately for Evgenia and Vladimir, there were several glaring errors in their free skate. But Eric simply refused to allow himself any emotional movement in any direction until the OAR athletes' final score was posted. Even though his brain registered the mistakes, and that likely meant he and Meagan were going to finish third, he needed to be 100 per cent sure. He laughs about how fidgety Meagan was beside him, often saying, 'Let me hope, I want to hope.'

"Maybe there was a millisecond of a flicker of, 'Oh my God, we're going to win another medal.' But I honestly quashed that thought immediately and kept myself completely numb until the marks came up.

"I was just sitting completely still and Meagan would say, 'Okay, I think we got it.'

"I said, 'Nope.' I refused to believe or even hope for anything until the marks were up and I saw my name on the screen. Meagan was saying, 'No, oh, let me hope. I want to hope.'

"It makes me laugh every time I watch it. Meagan and I are sincerely and genuinely happy for Aljona and Bruno. They've more than paid their dues. Aljona in her way and Bruno in his. We've toured with them. I consider them both my friends."

When the official results for the pairs were posted on the screen, there was joy and satisfaction. As Meagan says, "We had that great skate, and that was our beautiful Olympic moment. We didn't need a medal, but winning that bronze felt like a cherry on top of the cake after the performance we had. I felt proud and excited and in a bit of disbelief."

Eric too was feeling that heady mixture of disbelief, pure joy and surrealism. As they turned to each other to embrace and begin the celebrations, Meagan said, "We finally did it."

The placing of pairs on the Olympic podium was the exact same as it had been at the Grand Prix Final in December 2017, except that this time, Sui and Han were shedding tears of disappointment. They had finished their program strongly, beautifully, and perhaps they thought they had done enough to win, despite obvious errors at the top of the program. They scored 153.08, finishing less than point-five of a point in the combined scores lower than the German pair. Sui was sobbing in her partner Han's arms, overwhelmed by their near miss of Olympic gold.

Meagan says it was sad that Sui and Han weren't able to enjoy that moment like the bronze and gold medallists. "We tried to reassure them, telling them that they were so young and it would be their turn in four years for that gold medal. Later that evening, by the time we were getting our medals, they were feeling a lot better and a lot more positive."

In the meantime, the gold and bronze medallists appeared elegantly restrained in their joy. The restraint hinted at massive celebrations to come later, away from the prying cameras that follow figure skaters everywhere during the skating portion of the Olympics.

Meagan Duhamel and Eric Radford with Laura E. Young

They were taken directly from the medal ceremony to the mixed zone for interviews with all the television networks. Then it was Meagan's turn for drug testing. Eric had gone after the team event. She couldn't produce a sample so the drug testers followed her to the post-event press conference. Then Meagan had to go, saying, 'I'm going to pee my pants, let me go now.'

Eventually she finished the drug test, grateful that she was done with that aspect of her career. Athletes can never get comfortable with the process, she says. The testers have to see the athlete's entire body just in case the athlete is hiding something. It always seemed worse for Meagan who usually was so hydrated. Her samples would be diluted and she would have to wait and do another test. Then she'd be up all night.

Their Skate Canada media attaché guided Eric and Meagan that night, first to Canada House to celebrate with their families and share a champagne toast. They lingered for about an hour, and then headed off to the Medal Plaza in PyeongChang for the nightly official Victory Ceremony, where they would receive their medals and see their flag raised. According to the International Olympic Committee there were 103 of these ceremonies at the 2018 Games. Meagan says the athletes stand and wait for what seems like forever with athletes from other sports.

"The medal ceremonies were super exciting because we had already experienced it once. My thought during the team event ceremony had really come true. 'Three more days and you'll be back here.' It was true, it really worked out."

LOOKING BACK, MOVING FORWARD

Post-PyeongChang, Eric's tired face comes into view over Skype, from Montreal. It's a lucky ten minutes I have with someone who is interviewed out and about to get back on a plane to Australia.

After congratulating him I babble on about the good vibes in the air, a sense that all would end well for them at the games. Funny you should mention that, he says.

He relates how just prior to the games, he happened to get back in touch with his stepdaughter, Kina-Moon, daughter of his former partner Normand Piche. He had not seen Kina for nearly a year.

The three of them went for a coffee and caught up on their lives, how her school was going, what Eric had been up to. As Eric was about to head off, Kina tilted her head and said, "You're going to do amazing. I don't know why, I just had this thought that you're going to win."

Eric appreciated her support in a general way, but dismissed the premonition, saying "Oh, you never know what will happen." He promised to show off his medal the next time they met. It's a funny thing, though, he reflects, when people tell an athlete they have a feeling that things will go well for them. Eric would always shrug it off, perhaps not wanting to get anyone's hopes up. Yet, before the 2018 Olympics, many people approached him to say they had a good feeling about the games.

"A skater will come out at the beginning of the season and there's just something in the way they're skating. They build momentum and you can just sense it, in the way they perform. Meagan and I had this juxtaposition with how great the short debuted, and with how the Muse long program debuted."

Then their programs evened out and they found their way. Heading into the Olympics, they felt they were on the path and right where they needed to be. There was such a wash of relief for many in the skating world when they announced they were relaunching their Hometown Glory program.

Eric's favourite part of it all lies in knowing that they did indeed have a fairy-tale ending. He remembers all too well where they were in 2017. It all could have ended so differently and there would not have been the opportunities, the teaching, the shows, and even some prospects with his music that have since come down the pipe.

It almost feels like everything happened to another person named Eric Radford, he laughs.

Later we tag up again, this time he is in Mexico on a working vacation with his partner Luis Fenero. They have brought Eric's Olympic medals to show the adult skater he's training. The medals are solid, but the rest is a blur, as Eric's scratchy voice recalls.

"When I recall the performances, I remember how I was feeling rather than what we were doing. After the team long program, I remember thinking that I wanted to give the performance more in the individual event. I was happy with how the team skate went, but there was still room for me to feel more in the moment, and to release more, in the performance aspect. I felt that I did that in the individual event.

"When Meagan put her hands down on the triple Lutz, I remember thinking, 'Okay, okay next.' Maybe it would have been cool to have had the perfect program like we did in Boston in 2016, but the rest was so good that I don't ever think about that one little thing.

"When we came off the ice Bruno and Ian were both crying. I honestly can't remember exactly what Bruno said. I think it was, 'You guys were so amazing,' and he just kept repeating that. It really is a blur. Usually I can remember little details. I remember the moment we hit the ending position and Meagan crouched down into a little ball and we looked at each other.

"It usually takes a little longer for me to think back about everything that's happened. Then it slowly hits me. Then it really hits me. I remember thinking, 'Whoa. That was a really good skate. There was that one little thing on the Lutz and the rest was really good.' That's when it hit me: we just had a great skate at the Olympics. It all just happened. Then the next part, I hardly remember until we were back stage waiting for the Russians to skate."

Almost three months after the games, it was starting to really dawn on Eric—finally—what he and Meagan had accomplished. They attended the Skate Canada AGM where it felt like everyone who had ever followed their career was there. There was so much sincere pride in what Meagan and Eric had accomplished, he recalls.

"Meagan, Patrick and I had to give a little talk saying thank you. We each did it in slightly different ways. Then they showed a video afterwards. I never get extremely emotional, ever, but up on stage in front of all those people I was crying and I couldn't stop. It's hard to put into words. "It's like I got to see what we accomplished from everybody else's point of view for the first time.

"It made me think back to when Jamie and David won their gold medal in 2002 and when Elvis won his silvers in 1994 and 1998, and the way it made me feel inside even though at that time he had no idea who I was. But I felt like I was sharing it with him.

"When you're in the venue, the event doesn't feel very big. I think the Olympics feel bigger when you're watching it from home. It wasn't until I got home and people shared their experiences with me, that the feeling hit me and it was overwhelming. That's when I really, really felt the gravity, the weight, the importance of what that skate and what those medals really mean."

Eric says he and Meagan created a wave at the Olympics that they will ride for as long as they can, through shows, public events, speaking engagements, seminars, talks at schools. It all stems from that moment, that wave. They were also taking vacations and living their lives as they normally would, but a lot of what will happen in their lives will come from that Olympic moment.

And yes, he almost laughs in disbelief, it does indeed blow his mind that just about one year earlier, in the spring of 2017, they were leaving Richard and starting to work on a new short program with Julie and John. It is so funny how time can pass so fast and so slowly at the same time, he reflects. It feels like it was a whole other world then, or a whole lifetime ago, rather than one year.

At the Skate Canada AGM, Eric spoke with Sylvain, a Canadian judge, who had worked with Meagan and Eric much of the season. He had given them a lot of feedback and analysis and really was part of their journey to the podium. He was talking about when Meagan and Eric were skating to "Muse". Eric had almost forgotten he and Meagan had started the season with a totally different long program. It wasn't until the last two months of the season that they were skating to "Hometown Glory".

"They were probably the biggest highs and lows, and the most change, I've ever experienced in one season. For it to all happen and culminate with what happened at the Olympics—I don't even know the word to describe it.

"I feel just lucky, that we got lucky. Of course, we worked really hard, but it's almost fate that it all came together. There were so many variables, so many things could have gone wrong but didn't. It almost seems like it was meant to happen."

And yet, if Eric was to speak with skaters or any others who might only go to an Olympics to watch the competitions, he would say that he truly thinks he is proof that anyone can achieve any dream that one sets. Coming from a small town and moving away from home when he was thirteen—he spent a lot of time analyzing the exact mechanism that allowed him to accomplish everything he did.

"There has to be a certain amount of talent," he says, "but what's more important is the will and the grit to keep working hard when everything inside tells you to stop."

He speaks of taking baby steps towards a goal. Even if the baby steps are microscopic, after a certain amount of time and after you've taken a certain number of steps, you will be able to stop, turn around, and see the distance you've covered and know that you have moved towards reaching your goal. You just keep on going.

"I think whenever skating shows come up, Meagan and I will always be open and available to do them. Then I'll probably try to get my foot in the door with choreography and coaching. I like feeling free right now."

Post-Olympics, Meagan was feeling settled, even though she was busier than ever. Her medals were nestled in their boxes on the dining room table. Indulging me, she uses both hands to hold them up. They fill the computer screen. One side shows the Olympic rings, the other, the event they won. I joke that I expected her to be wearing all that bling. "They're so heavy, though," she laughs.

Elite athletes are a breed unto themselves. The medals matter but so does the performance in the moment. So, how does Meagan preserve that final skate for what it was without fussing about every other choreographed detail?

"The first time I watched our performance, I started thinking, 'That could have been better, let's fix this, let's fix that.' Then I realized we're not going to have another opportunity to do that.

"It was an amazing skate. I would rewatch it a few times to get my head away from the technical side. I mean, it's a shame about that triple Lutz in the final long program because I never missed it in the long program. I did the other three perfectly in the Olympics. In the grand scheme of things, it's still okay. Maybe if that hadn't happened, I wouldn't have been as sharp on the quad and the combination afterwards that are worth so many points.

"Normally, my analytical side would have nitpicked, 'Why did I do it? Oh no. Now I'm off. I'm going to miss everything.' Normally that's probably where my mind goes. In the past when I've made a mistake, everything tenses up. I didn't do that this time. Was it because of the mental state I was in? Probably. Was it because of how prepared we were physically and mentally going there? Probably.

"It was so scary calm before that long program in PyeongChang. I was so relaxed, I wondered if I was going to be able to do anything. I could never imagine that in the biggest moment of my life I'd feel so calm. But I did, and it all just linked together."

The entire season seemed to go as planned. They were always meticulous about their training, execution and planning over the years. Every season she and Eric skated together, they achieved all their goals, except in 2017. That's pretty spectacular when you think about it, she adds.

When the Olympics finished, Meagan wondered if she had created the perfect Olympic moment by envisioning exactly that, or was it fate, or was it just a random moment of luck that happened to descend and cloak their shoulders? It was exactly as she imagined it would be, leading her to wonder if the power of her own thoughts created that.

When Eric and Meagan were on the podium at the Grand Prix Final in December, Meagan had what seemed to be a gut feeling. Meagan hoped this would be the Olympic podium. And that is where they finished their career. They stood third with the Germans first and the Chinese second.

"We love Aljona and Bruno. We love Sui and Han. It's been the six of us for so long."

People have asked Julie Marcotte if she was disappointed that Meagan and Eric didn't win the gold medal in the individual pairs event. She wonders how anyone could be. Meagan and Eric did their best in an extremely strong field, she says. And at the start of the 2017–2018 season, Julie says it was absolutely possible they would not have even medalled at the Olympics.

But the team supporting the Olympic bronze medallists keeps pinching themselves, Julie says from her home in Montreal. "Moments like that, you don't have them a million times in your life. Everything worked out amazingly."

She recalls how it was in May 2017, when she was watching Meagan and Eric on a daily basis, and the skaters' working relationship was not great. They were never rude, and there was no fighting, but it was like they were speaking a different language. Perhaps their *politesse* made it worse, as they kept everything bottled up inside.

It was striking for Julie, who always talked about Eric and Meagan in seminars she would give, explaining how the two skaters always chose to see what was good about the other, how they worked out disagreements. In 2017 that ability was gone. Now they were focused on what they thought the other should do and what the other was not bringing to the team. And they seemed to be keeping their frustrations to themselves. They were in two different worlds.

Meagan had come to talk to Julie. Meagan didn't want to go through another season like that, Julie recalls. "Her body was tired. I don't think she ever meant that she wanted to stop skating. I just think it was her way of saying, emotionally, she was crying out for help."

The timing was strange to Julie because almost immediately after that meeting, she listened to April Meservy sing "With or Without You" for the first time.

Then, the CBC just happened to have a documentary film crew in the changeroom in Sainte-Julie that May day, recording the moment as Julie played the music for the skaters and coach Bruno.

"It was bizarre," Julie says. "We had to go listen to the music as if nothing was going on. But when I played the music it was an epiphany to them. It spoke to them. They both started to cry. All the words came out in the song and said what they wanted to say about each other and where they were at. In that moment they came back together."

Julie jokes lightly that even extensive therapy could not have brought Meagan and Eric back together as well as the magic of that moment in the dim lighting of an arena changeroom.

They already had that song on their skating to-do list, but not that specific version. Usually Julie listens to thirty different versions of a song, twenty seconds of each, listen, move on, listen, move on.

"I found this specific version. When I was in my studio listening to it, the song gave me shivers and brought tears to my eyes. I felt Meagan sing it. I don't know how to explain it."

Part way through the song, a man's voice comes in to support April's voice and that spoke to Julie as well. "I've been so emotionally connected to the two of them that it felt like it was their voices. After the year they'd had, the focus was on bringing them back to what made them special," Julie recalls.

Which is the long answer to how Julie felt when Meagan and Eric texted her from China in December 2017 to say they were dropping their wonky Muse long program to return to Adele and "Hometown Glory" for Canadians and the Olympics.

Julie supported them because she knew how far apart they had been. "Why would I object if they felt like it was going to put them in a better place? And it was one of our programs together as well. I felt emotionally attached to all their programs. Some of them good, some of them not so good, but every program they did helped them get to where they are today."

As Julie watched the final Olympic long program from Montreal, she inhaled when Eric and Meagan started and exhaled at the end. The field was so strong there was no room for error if Meagan and Eric wanted to land on the podium, she says.

"At the same time, for some reason I was not nervous. For some reason I knew they were going to skate well. All of those years, all of what they had done, the fact that they had faced difficult times and had come back up—I knew that in the given moment all of it was going to come together. I took in the moment and I was just wowed. At the same time it was a bittersweet feeling because they are moving on."

Like a proud mother, Julie was awash in emotion coming from a million angles, she says. She was seeing her skaters off, aware of what their impact on the sport will be.

"People who don't have the conventional match, they're always going to be able to identify with, and find strength in, the fact that Eric and Meagan twice were world champions." She reflects on the differences between the two skaters, size, style, approach—those differences can be inspirational for younger kids, she believes.

"When you find your own path, nothing is impossible. You just have to find your own path and your own signature, your own journey."

The post-Olympic transition continues and sometimes it's hard to believe skating life will continue after the sheer exhilaration of the Olympics. Bruno Marcotte is back coaching. Kirsten Moore-Towers and Michael Marinaro are back on the ice. Younger teams are moving to the school in Montreal, Bruno says. He may be back to coach the North Koreans. Everything seems back to normal and yet, roles are switching and evolving. Bruno is looking forward to a vacation with Meagan in Ireland, Scotland, and England, as he makes his own role switch to that of just husband. He jokes that he might miss giving Meagan and Eric "crap" when they come off the ice. Perhaps.

The season ended so well for his top pairs team because it started well, he believes. Their short program was well-received and that boosted their confidence. They fixed their issues with "Muse" and had a decent end to the Grand Prix season, on the podium yet again.

"But always there was a kind of a little doubt in their minds—did they have the right long program to compete and challenge the other teams? Not that they didn't score well, it's just about a feeling, the way they've evolved and matured over the years. There was never that full comfort level into the program. That resulted in a little bit of tension within the training," he says.

When Meagan called to tell him they were reviving their program to Adele's "Hometown Glory" for Canadians and the Olympics, he agreed with the decision and told everyone around them that it was something they felt they had to do.

"This is something they strongly feel as a team, as partners, as friends. At the end of the day it's not so much about the program but how they feel about the program. I think that really gave them the energy to move into the final stretch of the season. It gave them that common goal, that common feeling, that common trust that no matter what, they could overcome any obstacle."

Their programs were clean every day in practice, and Meagan and Eric wondered aloud if they were peaking too soon. Bruno told them about Alexei Yagudin, the 2002 Olympic men's champion from Russia. Bruno had worked at a seminar with Alexei years ago in Vancouver. "He's one of the greatest competitors I've ever seen. He was telling me that leading up to the Olympics, he did clean programs every day, for a month."

So he told Meagan and Eric they were ready and they were peaking just the way they should. "It's a statement about the training you've put in and your entire journey."

Of course the best laid training and preparation can shatter in the face of Olympic pressure. Bruno watched as the more Meagan and Eric competed, the better they felt.

They had calculated everything and taken everything into consideration. "Eric and Meagan, they love to stay in their routine and they have to follow exactly what is planned. If not, it's going to throw them off. But for some reason at the Olympics they were welcoming changes of plan. We made changes as the week went on, but there was no struggle.

"Once it starts going well there's a snowball effect. You become more and more confident. You start to think less and trust your training. The less you think, the better you can compete."

As the pair of eight years took to the ice, Bruno thought about the standing ovation the crowd had just awarded Aljona and Bruno, the world-record score the Germans had posted, and the fact that they had been in fourth behind Meagan and Eric after the short program.

"I just thought to myself, 'If Meagan and Eric can overcome this situation they deserve a medal, they deserve everything coming their way because this is not easy.'"

Meagan Duhamel and Eric Radford with Laura E. Young

And they were so on. He was able to live in the moment of the skate, not just get more nervous as the program went on. In a wash of bittersweet moments, he recalled the previous eight years.

"You want to finish on top. But it's also finished. It's over. That's it." He laughs lightly. "There's no better way to end up, but it's sad at the same time."

And, he remains singularly, fiercely proud of the way Meagan and Eric nailed the throw quad. The side-by-side Lutz got them noticed and was their signature element, but the throw quadruple Salchow made them champions, he says. "To land that throw quad at the Olympics was symbolic. That became their weapon of choice in the last couple of years."

They had started a trend but no one really came close to landing it, especially the way Meagan did in her final competitive program, as perfect as it could be, leaving no doubt for anyone, including the judging panel—"No review on that element," Bruno laughs. "No other team was able to perform it competition in and out. When it really mattered, to nail it on one foot like this, there was no better way to end it."

It sounds like another sports cliché, but it is true that in less than a year, Meagan and Eric went from the bottom to the top of the mountain, from being out of the Olympic medal chatter to taking home two Olympic medals.

In June of 2017 they were leaving a coach and a training site. Almost exactly one year later, they were back home in Northern Ontario, to experience true hometown glory.

In Red Lake, and still not believing it, Eric walks hand in hand with Luis like any other couple in love and enjoying the day, Red Lake's second Pride Day.

There is a newly minted sign proclaiming Eric Radford Way, the street where he grew up and where he will take Luis to show off his childhood home. The house is empty and up for sale but the daughter of the owners kindly opened the door and allowed all the Radfords and Luis the time to journey down memory lane together.

For Eric, skating was a home, a place that taught him to fly. Skating was also about music, he says.

"The combination of jumping and spinning while getting to dance to the music made the sport so fun and multi-dimensional. Now that my career is finished and I can look back at it as one complete unit, I know the reasons I started skating are the same reasons I continued on."

In 2006, he broke his toe and couldn't skate for six weeks. It was the longest block of time he was ever off his skates, throughout his lengthy skating career.

"I remember my first day back on the ice after all that time. I was just skating around the ice, feeling the wind in my hair and hearing it in my ears, listening to the sound my edges made and feeling the speed across the ice. The moments where I would lose myself in expressing the music and everything else just melted away created so many memories for me."

He may have thrown his partner Meagan to an Olympic first with the complex throw quadruple Salchow, but he appreciated the simple aspects of the sport, too. "These simple things were something I loved each time I skated and are what I will probably miss most when I hang up my skates for good."

Meagan's love for skating has also remained steady over the years. Through all the highs and lows, the fact remained that she loved to skate and that kept her going. Being at the rink was never a sacrifice. "I never once didn't want to go to the rink. Skating always drew me in and I always felt pure joy being at the rink to train or compete. The feeling of floating and flying across the ice, and overtop of Eric's head, is an indescribable feeling."

For Meagan there was always so much joy in working towards learning something new, and in feeling the adrenaline rush backstage before she stepped on the ice to compete.

She loved the struggle. How high could she bounce back after a fall? How could she make something happen that, perhaps in hindsight, was never meant to happen?

"How could I continue to turn my weaknesses into my strengths? Over time, I realized that this is what was most compelling about figure skating to me. It was the push. The drive to work towards something that most of the time seemed like an impossible task."

In Lively, there is an official celebration of all that Meagan has achieved. The gifts pile up in Meagan's arms: flowers from skaters at Walden and Copper Cliff Figure Skating Clubs; presents from local businesses. Athletes will skate and play in Meagan Duhamel's House, the long-awaited sign will fly high above the ice pad inside T.D. Davies Community Centre and Arena, home of the Walden Figure Skating Club, joining Jennifer Prouse's banner from the 1990 Canadian championships. The arena is just down the road and around the corner from where Meagan grew up at the corner of Irene Crescent and Turner Drive, now Meagan Duhamel Drive.

At that reception in June at her high school, Lively District, Meagan is more overloaded with hardware and gifts than she was coming home from the Olympics. She had managed to finish her Grade 12 year at home in Lively, although she didn't attend the graduation ceremony. On June 8, 2018, Meagan, Olympic and two-time world champion, even gets her high school grad moment as Principal Leslie Mantle positions a mortar board atop Meagan's head.

Her voice raw from talking to so many groups that week at home, Meagan speaks to the current crop of students of the role "old-fashioned hard work and dedication" played in her life, the value of teamwork, and the trust and belief she and Eric had in one another. She tells the students that she missed the Olympics twice before she managed to get there. "Keep your eye on the prize," she says.

At Lively High, a reception follows the official ceremony and someone has produced a vegan cake option in short order, to go with the larger slab cake for the students.

Way northwest, Balmertown-Red Lake unveils a cupcake cake that celebrates Eric Radford Way.

In their respective small hometowns Meagan and Eric do the honours, cutting the cake to both celebrate one life and the next as they move forward and onward. There is cake for everyone.

References

In writing this book, Laura relied extensively on interviews in-person, via Skype, and over the phone with Meagan, Eric, Heidi and Danny Duhamel, Valerie and Rick Radford, Julie Marcotte, and Bruno Marcotte. Richard Gauthier did not wish to be interviewed for the story.

As well, Laura caught Grand Prix and the Olympic 'PyeongChang flu,' watching every figure skating competition available and all but wearing out the PVR reviewing recordings. Special credit to CBC's short documentary, Beyond the Limits, (Meagan and Eric). https://watch.cbc.ca/media/media/short-docs/beyond-the-limits-megan-and-eric/38e815a-00dc9ea3a53

Interior Photo Credits

Danielle Earle, Heidi and Danny Duhamel, Meagan Duhamel, Eric Radford, Valerie and Rick Radford, Laura E. Young

Bibliography

Brasseur, Isabella, & Lloyd Eisler, as told to Lynda D. Prouse. *Brasseur & Eisler: To Catch a Dream*. Macmillan Canada, 1996.

Brennan, Christine. *Edge of Glory The Inside Story of the Quest for Figure Skating's Olympic Gold Medals*. A Lisa Drew Book (Scribner), 1998.

Hamill, Dorothy & Deborah Amelon. *A Skating Life: My Story*. Hyperion 2007.

Flemming, Peggy & Peter Kaminksy. *The Long Program: Skating Toward Life's Victories*. Pocket Books, 1999.

Milton, Steve. *Skate Talk: Figure Skating in the Words of the Stars*. Key Porter Books, 1997.

Milton, Steve. *Figure Skating's Greatest Stars*. Firefly Books Ltd., 2009.

Orser, Brian & Steve Milton. *Orser: A Skater's Life*. Key Porter Books, 1988.

Smith, Beverley. *Gold on Ice: The Salé and Pelletier Story*. Key Porter Books, 2002.

Smith, Beverley. *Skating to Sochi*. Lulu.com 2013.

Smith, Beverley & Dan Diamond. *A Year in Figure Skating*. McClelland & Stewart, 1997.

Thomas, Kelti. *How Figure Skating Works*. Maple Tree Press, Toronto, 2009.

Virtue, Tessa, Scott Moir & Steve Milton. *Tessa & Scott: Our Journey from Childhood Dream to Gold*. House of Anansi Press Inc., Toronto, 2010.

Stay in touch with Meagan on her website lutzofgreens.com. Stand by for Eric's transition to composer. You will literally be hearing from him.

Both of them.

Author Acknowledgements

Meagan

I'd love to send a huge thank you to everyone that made this book happen, especially to Laura Young for taking on the job of writing and Latitude 46 for their work publishing the book.

Of course, I'd like to extend a thank you to Eric, because without him by my side all these years, our story wouldn't be what it is. I could never have imagined everything that lay ahead of us when we began skating together in March 2010.

Thank you to my many coaches who have been part of my journey, from the Walden Skating Club to Mariposa School of Skating to my training sites in Montreal. Everyone's guidance and expertise allowed me to grow into such a successful figure skater.

I'd like to extend a thank you to my competitors, training mates and friends, who made my experiences in this sport both beautiful and challenging. You all pushed me beyond my limits, and for that I am grateful.

I would like to sincerely thank our families for all of their support and help throughout this incredible journey. All that you have given and shared never went unnoticed and has been greatly appreciated.
Special thanks to my family for putting me on the ice at such a young age, for encouraging me that anything is possible and for teaching me the values of hard work and dedication.

Eric

I would like to thank my parents and my family for their relentless support of me while I pursued my dreams.

To my partner and husband, Luis Fenero, for sharing and amplifying the most amazing moments in my life.

To my first skating coach, Debra Geary, for instilling the love of skating in me and teaching me to believe in myself.

To Paul Wirtz for making me the skater and most importantly the competitor I am today.

To the team of coaches that brought Meagan and me from the very beginning to the top of the world: Bruno Marcotte, Julie Marcotte, Sylvie Fullum, Richard Gauthier, and Ian Connolly.

To my friends whom I consider to be some of the most important people in my life and who lived my ups and downs with me.

And of course I thank Meagan, the biggest fan of skating I know, who never settled for anything less than her best and whose dedication inspired me to be my best every day.

Laura E. Young

To my parents Carolyn (Roberts) and Michael Young and mother-in-law Vanda (Simon) Gregoris; my extended family, especially: Iva; Robbie, Chelsie, Jon, Pam, and the grand-ones, and James, and our own Erik and Meghan and their parents, Douglas, Catherine and Howard.

My friends, especially Jen, and Evelyn and her husband Kerry, for a long-ago wedding gift of beautiful book ends and Kerry's hope that one day my books would rest between them. Research assistants extraordinaire Heidi Duhamel and Valerie Radford and the Duhamel and Radford families, and Maxine Connolly. Richard Radford for photos.

Meagan, Eric and the team in Montreal for fitting this project into their crazy schedules to achieve this book.

Latitude 46 publishers Laura and Heather; the deft guiding hand-eye coordination of editor Morgan Grady-Smith; the wonderful souls at DBS Computers and the South Branch of the Sudbury Library; and my inspiring students and colleagues at Cambrian College.

Teammates at Laurentian Masters Swimming and the Lake Nepahwin Swimmers (#swimdrinkfish); the lifeguard team at R.G. Dow Pool; the marvellous Sudbury sports community (Sudbury Rocks), and my journalism colleagues for all their work;

And to Roberto, Glen and Neal in the canoe with the keys, a towel, and tea.

Photo: Brent Wohlberg

LAURA E. YOUNG

Laura E. Young is a journalist based in Sudbury and the author of the award-winning Solo Yet Never Alone Swimming the Great Lakes. A graduate of the University of Kings College in Halifax, N.S., she has worked in various media in Northern Ontario and has won awards for sports, feature, and spot-news writing through the OCNA. She teaches in Cambrian College's public relations program and is a certified lifeguard, swimmer and advocate for water quality and safety.

Printed by Imprimerie Gauvin
Gatineau, Québec